JUDICIAL
TERRORISM

JUDICIAL TERRORISM

BIG-TIME CORRUPTION
IN SMALL-TOWN AMERICA
A TRUE STORY

CATHY THOMPSON LANGELLA

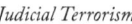
Cover design by Bill Francis Peralta

Finally, for Jody,
my sweet little black-and-white furbaby,
who was always innocent, always loving,
and always knew, every day,
that I would come home to take care of her

Power tends to corrupt,
and absolute power corrupts absolutely.
Great men are almost always bad men.

—Lord Acton (1834–1902)

Contents

Judicial Terrorism

You may find it hard to believe that the Constitution of the United States does not always protect us. We are not all afforded "constitutionally protected" rights in this country.

The entire time my life was being ravaged by both elected and appointed officials, I believed that it was a given that the Constitution would afford me equal protection under the law and due process. I was sure that eventually my abusers would be called to account, that they would have to face some kind of justice for what they had done.

What I learned was that elected and appointed officials, as well as others who have been entrusted with responsibilities and power, are absolutely immune from any kind of punishment, accountability or justice. They are the ultimate protected class.

I also learned that being a middle-aged white woman in the United States of America is not only *not* a protected class but that I was "sh*t out of luck" because I *was* a middle-aged white woman. I was devastated to learn that if I had been a member of any minority group—black, Hispanic, Muslim, gay, or transgender—law firms would have been beating down my door, begging to represent me, and I would have been awarded a multimillion-dollar settlement a long time ago.

This country has become a dangerous place for those of us who aren't minorities, and for those of us who don't have vast financial resources. We are just out of luck, and in very real danger.

The Rape: A Backdrop

THIS IS NOT a sob story. Like you, I have a life story, and I will include here only what I feel is absolutely relevant. It is important to me that you have context, that you understand the backdrop of my experiences before I was determined to be a "nonentity" in our local judicial system. I have spent a lifetime making mistakes, making terrible choices and attempting to learn from those mistakes and choices. I have also had many blessings in my life, and have learned that we take way too many of them for granted. Especially in this country. Especially in the United States of America.

~ ~ ~

I was brutally raped when I was nine years old by a young man who lived in my neighborhood. I was walking home from piano lesson, like so many little girls do, and he grabbed me from the sidewalk and took me into his house. More than fifty years later, I can still recall every sight and sound, every word from his mouth, what he looked like and what he did to me. I was able to identify him, and my parents took me to confront his parents in the same house where I'd been raped hours before. In 1961, it wasn't like it is today. There were no "victim's rights" or rape counselors or much of anything for a victim. Especially not for a child.

And because things were so different back then, he was never charged with anything, I was never given any counseling or support to help me try to deal with it, and my parents never spoke of it to me again, ever.

~ ~ ~

When I was in my early teens, I learned that my mother never wanted kids. She would often tell us she wasn't cut out to be a mother, and didn't really want children. She actually told us that. Although there were different forms of birth control, even in the 1950s, my mother and my father had *five* children. Five children my mother didn't want.

Also in my early teens I figured out that I was born six and a half months after my parents were married, and asked my mother if she had sex with my father before they were married. I remember well my mother laughing and telling me that her wedding night was one of the "biggest disappointments" of her life because my father was a virgin, and he "didn't know what to do." She told me she cried herself to sleep on her wedding night.

For a few years, the biggest mystery to me in my sheltered life was how I weighed nine pounds, thirteen ounces at birth after a six-and-one-half-month pregnancy. My younger sister would eventually explain to me a "secret" she told me my mother had confided to her when we were both in our twenties.

My mother had appropriate schooling at Bryn Mawr and Smith College, and was groomed to move to New York City, which she did; get a job, which she did; and find a professional man that could give her a "good life." My sister told me our mother was engaged to a man who was well-to-do—and Jewish—and that he made the fatal mistake of striking my mother during an argument. I was told she immediately called off the engagement and broke off the relationship. She also almost immediately found herself pregnant and no longer engaged.

The man that I always knew as Dad had dated my mother in their hometown before she went to New York City, and he had always cared for her. So the story goes that my mother contacted her former beau, my dad, and the family arranged a very speedy wedding at her family's home.

Unfortunately for my mother, she had been doing all the right things to put herself on a path to higher society and money, had an exciting career on Wall Street where she had already made a name for her young self (she was twenty-five); and a baby (me) ruined all her plans, and all of her life. She ended up returning to her hometown, where there was little higher society and no New York City life, and she was now married to a man she didn't love, and had a baby she didn't want. And then had four more children in ten years.

When I first learned this story from my sister, I was really angry. I was in my twenties, and felt really cheated. I'm not sure what I felt I was cheated out of, but that's how I felt. As I got older, I felt really sad, mostly for my mother. Although I confronted her twice over the course of my life, she would never admit to a thing, and would only spew venom at my sister, calling her a liar. My mother was never happy a day in her life after me. I am sure of that.

~ ~ ~

When I was barely thirteen, the boy I was "dating" taught me everything he thought I should know about having sex, and also taught me that you could be "loved" and be occasionally battered, and that there was no contradiction there. Early on in our "relationship," I confided to him about the rape, and it turned out to be a big bonus for him, because he was able to repeatedly throw it in my face whenever he felt like calling me a "whore" or a "slut."

"I'll bet you liked it, didn't you?" And, "Just how big was it? Was he bigger than me? Was he better than me?"

And just like the typical victim, I came to believe it was my fault, and also believed what he told me. I was lucky that he "loved" me, because no one else would want me anyways. And if he had to smack me around, well, that was just to keep me in line, or teach me a lesson. I spent most of my junior high and high school years being used for sex and battered simultaneously. He introduced me to cutting, and several times we both took razor blades to our arms and wrists. I guess the goal was always to cut enough to draw blood, but not enough to kill yourself. Looking back on this bizarre—and dangerous—activity, I have no idea why we did it.

Because my parents hated him, and because he had smashed down doors in their house and broken furniture with me sitting in it, and because they had seen and heard him abuse me, I thought they were being totally unreasonable, and just knew I had to get out of their house.

When I was seventeen I ran away from home with my abuser and thought I had finally achieved my dream. I was going to have a home and a family of my own. I couldn't wait to have kids. I couldn't wait to take care of someone and be loved. How in the hell I thought I'd get there is baffling, but I know it was how I felt. I wanted desperately to be pregnant since I was about fifteen and was ecstatic when I finally was, at seventeen.

Yep, it was insanity. Just the beginning of more insanity than I could ever imagine.

I had two daughters by the time I was twenty, and I loved them more than anything in my life. We had our own apartment and some crappy furniture, and often not much food. But he worked and paid the bills and only beat me occasionally, and only when I deserved it. Like when his breakfast wasn't timed to the minute and he would come downstairs from his shower to find not-hot-enough coffee. Sometimes he would throw the coffee at me, and sometimes he would flip the entire breakfast table upside down and leave me on the floor to clean it up. After pummeling me with his fists on the back of my head and neck. Always so the bruises weren't so obvious to anyone else.

At one point, when my children were about two and four, I was working full-time and coming home to do the housework and take care of my daughters. He was not working, and was often full of rage. When I was exhausted and desperately in need of sleep, he would often scream at me to "stay awake!" or "Don't you dare go to sleep on me!" and he would put his foot in the small of my back and push me off the bed onto the floor. When I would cry and go into my daughters' bedroom, to try to sleep at the bottom of their bed, he would often drag me off that bed by my arm or sleeve, pulling me onto the floor, often kicking me.

When I could no longer stomach sex, he occasionally raped me, and I learned to close my eyes and try to think of anything else in the world to get through it. I had nowhere to go, and no money. He would threaten to kill me if I ever took his kids from him, and would routinely dismantle the car's engine when he was afraid I would try to leave with them.

One lucky day, when I was all of twenty-six, he told me he was leaving me. He'd found a lovely woman who worked at the same factory, and he screamed at me, in front of our house, in public for everyone to hear, "She gives much better blow jobs than you ever did!" And then he left me.

Thank God for her! She has been his wife for more than thirty years, so I guess he was right.

~ ~ ~

I was finally free of the torment, and now I was terrified on a different level. I had to figure out a way to support myself and my two children, and had spent almost all the time since they were born taking care of them and our home and their father. After we separated and then divorced, he was able to avoid paying child support for more than ten years by lying about what he earned and working under the table. When my daughters visited him on weekends and vacations, he would buy them bicycles and new clothes and toys that I could never afford, and they loved it.

Well, even though I wasn't praying for an answer—because I was ignorant—into my life came my second knight in shining armor. I met a nice guy in a bar, drunk out of his mind, and, within a week, let him move in with us. It took me a while to understand what alcoholism really is, because I had never been exposed to it, and it took me years longer to understand what it could do to me. Especially what it could do to my daughters.

I had spent so many years being so beaten down—physically, mentally, and emotionally—and I had absolutely no self-esteem left, if I ever had any to begin with. So when Knight in Shining Armor No. 2 said he loved me, and then left me to go on benders and drank up all our money, and knocked me down and punched me in the face and threatened to slit my throat, and then cried afterward, begging for forgiveness, well, it just made sense to me that he must really love me, or he wouldn't keep coming back, right? And how lucky could one woman be?

I learned that his father had died at the age of thirty-eight following surgery to try to repair a body that had literally been rotting away. He told me his father's alcohol addiction was so severe that he had resorted to drinking aftershave, as well as straining antifreeze through a piece of bread, just to get the alcohol from it when he couldn't afford to buy any. His father was a full-blooded Native American Indian, and alcoholism was rampant in their family, and on their home reservation in Canada.

We were married after "dating" for two years, and divorced five years after that. Our "honeymoon" in Toronto consisted of a nice hotel room in the middle of the city, where he ordered porn movies and repeatedly called me a slut, insisted we go to a porn shop so he could check out sex toys (although I had no idea what they were or what they were for), and literally tried to abandon me in a mall. He kept trying to distract me with something and then run from me, saying he was going to leave me in Toronto so he could get his freedom back. I found myself running at top speed through a shopping mall, chasing my new husband, begging him not to leave me there. What I did not understand at the time was that, because he was dry, trying to stay away from alcohol, trying to prove to me that he wasn't an alcoholic, he was going through horrific withdrawal, and I was experiencing the ravages of that withdrawal.

The car we were driving on our honeymoon was mine before I met him, and he told me that he was just as entitled to it as I was, since we were married. He would later tell me that he had planned to drive me out into the woods somewhere and leave me without my blood pressure medication so I would eventually die from "something." After more than a year of counseling and Al-Anon meetings, I learned that he saw me as the only person on the face of the earth that stood between him and his next drink because I desperately tried to help him get sober. In his mind, I was the "enemy," and his addiction convinced him that he absolutely had to get rid of me. Permanently.

No one can ever make someone else get sober. No one can ever make someone else feel anything. Your intentions can be the absolute best, but you cannot *ever* change someone's heart. You cannot *ever* change another person's *anything*.

To his credit, after days of terrorizing my daughters and me while on yet another bender, he checked himself into an inpatient drug and alcohol treatment facility, and he not only got sober, but he remained sober. He has not had a drink in more than thirty years. He has a beautiful wife and has a good job as a D&A counselor. We live in the same city, share the same faith, and are honestly friends today.

One of many miracles in my life, for sure.

~ ~ ~

Unfortunately, I had not become wiser, and would yet go through two more devastating relationships, both of which I thought were going to last a lifetime. (Yes, I was still that stupid.)

Near the end of marriage number 2, a deacon in our church had offered to give my husband and me marriage counseling sessions because we were in big trouble. He didn't know how to be a husband, and I was painfully unhappy and desperately lonely. Our "counselor" would soon admit to me that he was in love with me (yes, of course, he was married and had kids), and that he couldn't stand to see me being mistreated, so he wanted to take me away from all of my pain and give me a good life with lots of love and security. He said he hadn't had a real marriage for years, that his wife mistreated him—all the stereotypical lies. He wanted our kids to be part of our future family together, and convinced me to move to Raleigh, North Carolina, with him.

I made arrangements for my daughters to be taken care of until we both got work and could send for them. We both got decent jobs right away, got a nice little rental, and after three weeks, he told me he was convinced God was going to kill him if he didn't take me back home and go back to his wife. I would later find out that he was a sex addict and a pervert who had been having regular phone sex with the church pianist, also married with kids, among many other "hobbies."

Go figure. He had convinced me that it was God's will that we were together, and I guess I thought he was a prophet.

~ ~ ~

After going back to live with my parents (I refused to go back to Knight No. 2), I got a new job and a new apartment for my girls and me shortly after that. I believed it was going to be a new start for all of us, and I was optimistic. Shortly after starting my new job, my new boss started pursuing me, very romantically, and asked me out to dinner. He was separated from his wife and had three young children, who lived more than three hours away. His wife had left him for another man—a friend of his—and their third child was the result of her affair. He was smart and funny and passionate, and he loved me. I thought I'd finally found the Love of My Life. We worked so well together, and my kids really liked him. We would talk for hours about how we were going to have all our children together in a home somewhere on the New England coast, and how we were going to live happily ever after. I could not believe how happy I was, and I especially could not believe that any man could ever treat me so well, with so much respect and with such kindness.

And then one day his wife called him. She was hysterical and was begging him to reconcile. Their two young sons, both adolescents, were struggling terribly in school and missed their dad so much. They were devastated that their parents were apart. Because they lived several hours away, he only saw his kids most weekends, and he was grief-stricken.

And so he did the "right" thing. He told me he had to think of his children first, and he just couldn't live with himself if he didn't at least try to give them what they wanted. He left me more than devastated—he left me wanting to die. I just didn't think I was going to survive more pain. I wasn't going to commit suicide, but I often asked God to take my life and end my grief. I was so tired of being given hope and wanting so much to have a family. I wanted so much to have happiness and security and peace in my home, and it just would never come.

He would call me in the middle of the night, sobbing, telling me how much he loved and missed me. For a few weeks I still had to go to my job and try to avoid seeing him during the day. It was more pain than I could handle, but I just kept doing my job the best I could because I literally had no other options short of suicide. I desperately needed the job because I needed the money to pay our rent and try to take care of my daughters.

That is, until the day the owner of the company called me into his office and told me that he was going to have to let me go because he knew that my relationship with my boss had ended and it was just too "inappropriate" for me to stay on. He couldn't let my boss go; he was too important to the company. I had spent months learning every aspect of the business and was always told I was doing such a good job. During our peak season, I had worked twenty-one long days straight without a day off and ended up in the ER so sick I could barely stand up. But I was very happy working alongside the man I was going to spend the rest of my life with, so it didn't matter.

And then I got tossed to the curb, thrown under the bus, put out with the trash. And I decided I'd never, ever trust another man as long as I lived.

What happened to me back then would never happen today. Well, if it did happen today, at least I'd most likely own the company after suing both my boss and the owner. Things are much, much different today.

~ ~ ~

Several months later, I found a new job—one that I really enjoyed. I was working at a medical lab doing data entry and was known to my coworkers as a woman who had finally committed to never being in a serious relationship again. I was going to live the rest of my life taking care of myself and my daughters the best I possibly could, and would never trust another man again. Never, never, never!

My best friend of thirty years introduced me to a local attorney I'd never heard of, and we hit it off. Way too serious. Way too fast. Way too stupid. He was so nice and so kind and so flattering, and wanted to save me from all my bad memories and the pain I was still trying to work through. He couldn't believe that I had ever been treated badly, and was so sorry I'd ever been used and hurt and abused. He was going to show me a different life, a better life, one with a man who was going to be totally committed to me and would take care of me and love me.

He moved into my house about a week after our first date. He took me to Long Island to meet his parents after a couple of months of dating. He proposed with a diamond ring, and we were married four months after we met.

Yes, it's true. I *am* a genius.

I wanted to believe, with all of my heart, that this man was going to really, truly be my knight in shining armor. He said he was. Maybe he even wanted to be. But I didn't know so many things about him that I should have known, and it turned out to be the most dangerous relationship of my life.

More than a year after we got married, my husband's secretary quit to take another job closer to her home. We discussed our options at length and agreed that he would teach me the ins and outs of legal secretarial work, and we'd see if we could handle spending that much (way too much) time together. Yes, it's true, I am a genius.

Addictions

P/M/S ADDICTIONS. PORNOGRAPHY/MASTURBATION/SEX addictions. I brought them into my home and married them. In the beginning, I had no idea how bad they could be, or how sick the man was, or how dangerous and deadly the situation could become.

At first I dismissed finding the hidden magazines in my house, and just repeated—and repeated—that I would not have anything like that in my home, and that he had to get rid of it. In the beginning, he would promise me he "wouldn't do it again." Wouldn't buy it, wouldn't bring it home, wouldn't look at it. Those promises became meaningless, and I honestly believe he meant to keep them in the beginning. He wanted to know how to be a good husband and stepfather, or so he said, but he seemed to be struggling greatly.

I didn't know at the time what a sociopath was or what a narcissist was. I had married them too.

Sociopath: A person with a personality disorder manifesting itself in extreme antisocial attitudes and behavior and a lack of conscience.

Narcissist: A person who is overly self-involved, and often vain and selfish.

The psychoanalysis: A person who suffers from narcissism, derives erotic gratification from admiration of his or her own physical or mental attributes.

Over the course of many years, the hiding and the lies got worse. As with absolutely every addiction there is, P/M/S addictions are progressive. What gives you a thrill today isn't going to be good enough next month, or next year. Maybe it won't be good enough tomorrow.

I would believe that he had stopped, and wouldn't even be looking for any signs that he hadn't stopped. I wanted to believe, and believe *in*, my husband. I desperately wanted the marriage to work, and to be happy and content and spend the rest of my life with someone that loved me, wanted to take care of me, wanted to be taken care of by me. But I would be cleaning the house, or looking for something of mine, and out of an end table or a magazine would fall pictures or clippings. There would be confrontations and screaming and crying and apologies, and yet another "I didn't realize how upset this made you" (for the two hundredth time).

After some years, though, the attitude of the addict will ultimately change. It was no longer "I'm sorry, I won't do it again." It became "Why don't you get over it? I'm not hurting anybody! Everyone does it! You are just sick to make such a big deal out of this!"

Next, it was laughing at me, telling me, "You need help" and that *he* didn't have a problem, I did. That was partly true. Although he did have a problem, my problem was that I needed to be able to get myself out of this disaster, and I couldn't.

~ ~ ~

You see, over a period of many years, "we" had started taking in rescues. Cats and kittens that had been abused, neglected, abandoned, or were going to be destroyed. My husband had been raised with animals—both cats and dogs—and his mother always had quite a few at one time. I had been an animal lover since I was a small child, and would drag home anything that would let me. (I think there may be something to psychoanalyze here.) I always wanted to "save" an animal I saw as helpless and innocent.

If I caught a glimpse of a homeless cat downtown in the middle of winter, I would drive down there in a snowstorm and wait for hours with food and a humane trap, to try to rescue it. I did just that numerous times a block away from the police station, and was often watched like I was some kind of nutcase. Maybe so.

If a neighbor moved away and left their cat on their porch, I would watch it for days before realizing it had no food and no home, and then we would bring it in. It broke my heart dozens of times to see an animal that thought it had a family stare longingly, day after day, at a door that was never going to open for them. And they just wouldn't give up or leave. They were so committed to their family and just believed, I'm sure, that their mama or daddy would come back for them.

We had moved to a neighborhood just down the street from a cemetery, and I soon discovered that local scumbags would drop off unwanted cats and kittens in that cemetery, believing they would fend for themselves so much better there. You know, the cemeteries that have warm blankets and heaters and fresh water and food and all that great stuff?

If I looked outside in the bad weather and saw an animal that looked like it was starving and homeless, I would try to bring it inside. I never said no, and my husband knew it. So when the feral cats from the cemetery started having litters of kittens, he brought in several. Not several kittens, several litters. At one point, I was trying to dropper-feed several litters of kittens four or five times a day, some in separate bedrooms, some in carriers I had lined up on our dining room table, some in a baby playpen I'd covered with a sheet, some in our outbuilding in the backyard inside a small nylon tent. I'd make little litter boxes out of plastic storage containers and make up batches of kitten formula.

I'd force Nutri-Cal down their throats and help them learn to eat Kitten Chow and canned food.

During this time, I was working full-time at my husband's law office, and doing one hundred percent of the housework and dishes and laundry and litter box scooping. I just did what I felt had to be done, every single day; and my husband continued to do his thing. I had learned that he didn't particularly care much for being a lawyer, and although he could be a very, very good lawyer, his heart often wasn't in it. He had admitted to me that *his* dream was never to be a lawyer, that the dream was his father's. He wanted to go into urban planning, but his father strongly suggested that he change his mind. And since his father was helping him financially, he did.

~ ~ ~

I started to learn more and more about P/M/S addictions, and at one point, my husband not only admitted that he had serious problems, but he joined an online "no-porn" support group, where he bared his soul to other addicts, and then would ask me to read what he had written, or what was being written on the site by other members, to help *me* understand what he was going through, and what he was trying to deal with. He admitted to his support group that he had destroyed our marriage, that I had been a good wife to him and was always there for him, and that he felt tremendous guilt about what he had been doing.

The things that I read written by other addicts literally made me sick to my stomach. There was perversion out there that I had never heard of. There were also hundreds of posts from the significant others of the addicts who talked about their own anguish and feelings of helplessness, and a lot of them talked about loving the addict but wanting out. Just like me.

My husband's online support group affiliation and attempts at sobriety lasted less than six months. And his addictions didn't pick up where they'd left off, but had apparently accelerated. He would later admit to me that pornography was the first thing he thought about when he woke up, and the last thing he thought about when he tried to fall asleep. He thought about other women—other women, naked—constantly, all day, every day. He told me he would have to imagine that I was someone else to have sex with me. (I do not call it making love when a person isn't capable of loving someone.)

I discovered hard-core porn movies downloaded into his office computer, and I knew that he often met with children in his office when their families were involved with Children and Youth Services, and it scared the hell out of me. I would also later discover that he would look at porn on his laptop while sitting in our family room only a few feet away from me and I was oblivious to it.

I discovered links to teen porn in his e-mail and knew that in Pennsylvania, that would be considered child porn.

That not only scared the hell out of me, but it made me so sick I can't begin to describe it. I not only had daughters, but I had a granddaughter, and we were always around young women at work.

~ ~ ~

I WAS SO desperate to find a way to be able to get out. I had been working in my husband's law office for more than fifteen years, and I also knew I'd never be able to get another legal secretarial job in our area. I knew everyone, and knew too much *about* everyone. I knew I had to try to do something different. I couldn't just pack up dozens of rescues and cart them off somewhere. And I damn well knew my husband would never take care of any of them.

I had always loved redecorating the homes we'd lived in, was pretty good at painting and wallpapering, and had learned to use quite a few tools. I had been watching HGTV for years and had picked up a zillion tips on redecorating and remodeling. I had already designed our family room addition and the new kitchen and bathroom myself, and I thought our house was beautiful. I was sure I could learn more and, if given the chance, might be able to make some money doing it on my own.

I convinced my husband that it would be a great way to supplement our income, and at the same time, it would get me away from him during the day. We had spent nearly twenty-four hours a day together for years, and it was way too much, even in the healthiest relationship. His work could be extremely stressful, for both of us, and we had to go home together after stressing all day. My daughter had already been working for us full-time for several years, and I knew she could pretty much run the office herself if she had to. I told them both that I would still come in to the office to put things together that she didn't feel comfortable with, and it sounded like a good plan.

We were able to buy two distressed properties, one bank-owned, over the course of a year or so. They both pretty much needed gutting and total renovation, but we made a deal with my daughter and her husband that they would help us on the weekends, and when it came time to sell the house after it was done, we would split the profits. We would borrow the money for the purchase and renovations, and if we needed more, my husband and I would put it in ourselves. They wouldn't have to put up any money, just substantial time and work. My son-in-law had proven himself to be very talented at just about any remodeling job that would need done, and over the course of many months, he also taught me to do a lot more. I had my own air compressor and framing nailer, and I not only learned framing, but I loved it.

Since I was spending more and more time away from the office, I was not only much happier, but I thought that my husband seemed to maybe even be relieved that we weren't together as much. He would later admit that the biggest reason he was very glad I was away from the house so often was because he had more time to indulge in his favorite hobbies.

During this time, I would only go to the office when I needed to put some legal paperwork together that my daughter couldn't, or to pay bills. I meticulously kept track of all our bills, both personal and business, and knew what amounts were due on what dates. I knew my husband would go into a rage if anyone ever called about an overdue bill, no matter what it was, so I always made sure things were paid on time, or early.

When money came into the office that clients had paid for fees, the funds would get deposited, and I would draw from them to pay the bills. My husband also had a biweekly paycheck for his salary from the county, both for being chief public defender and for working for CYS; and because his paycheck never covered all the bills for both our home and office building, I would also draw from the escrow account when he had done work for clients and they had paid a retainer. My daughter would usually tell me when someone had money on deposit, and it was working out really well. We always seemed to have enough to cover everything, so everything was paid on time, and we didn't get collection calls.

~ ~ ~

One afternoon, I stopped in at the office to check on things and pay some bills, and I overheard my daughter on the phone talking to another law office about money we had on deposit from a real estate transaction that had closed a year before. I didn't know exactly how much money we had on deposit, because I wasn't paying much attention to the bank statements. All I knew was that there wasn't as much as she was saying we were holding.

I remember feeling as though my entire head and face had gone numb. I just sat there and told myself to keep breathing. I could not have possibly heard her say that we were holding a substantial amount of someone else's money. That could not have been what I heard!

When she was off the phone, I tried to calmly ask her what she meant by money we were holding. She told me that a transaction had closed the year before, and because there was never a recorded satisfaction for one mortgage, we were holding the proceeds in escrow until they provided us with a satisfaction. I told my daughter that there was no way we had that much money in the account, and she told me she knew that. I asked her why she didn't tell me that we were supposed to be holding a certain amount of money for this deal, and the only thing she said was, "I thought you knew."

Oh my God! *This cannot be happening!* My life was surely going to be over. Like right now! I had been working so hard and had so much hope that I was finally going to find a way out, and now I was going to find myself dead at the hands of my husband, or maybe something even worse.

I was literally in a state of 24/7 panic for several weeks. I had no idea what to do. I had no idea how to replace that kind of money. The houses we were renovating were going to take so long to finish, and there was no way I'd see any profit from any of my work for many months.

I tried to think of anyone I knew that had enough money to help me with a loan. I had two cousins—one in California who had started a foundation in Los Angeles and one in Texas who was a multimillionaire by virtue of his connections and law license. I wrote to them, and the California cousin told me he didn't have that kind of money. The millionaire Texas lawyer told me the best thing for me to do was to tell my husband and then go with him to the district attorney and just "be honest" about what had happened. He told me he was sure they would find a way for us to pay it back, make restitution, not face any charges. He told me that I would be surprised if I ever knew how many times "things like that" have happened with lawyers he knew himself.

I knew that my husband would never have any part in what he was suggesting, and I also knew that my husband would make my life a living hell forever if he knew what I had done.

So, because I am a genius (previously established), I decided the best way out was to win enough money to replace what I apparently had taken that wasn't mine. More than a year before this, my husband and I used to go to a casino every once in a while on an Indian reservation about twenty miles from our home. Sometimes, when he didn't feel like going, or when he thought I seemed to be overworked and too stressed, he would encourage me to go with a friend or by myself. In one six-week period, I had amazingly won $12,000 *three different times*, for a total of $36,000, in less than two months. We had used a lot of the money to help pay for renovations on our home.

So here I was, honestly believing I was facing death, and panic-stricken beyond description. I just tried to convince myself that if I really set my mind to it, I could win enough to replace whatever was missing. I hadn't been going to the casino much anymore because I was working almost all the time, and now I was going to have to get serious about winning something big.

Every time I had enough money, I would go to the casino; but because there wasn't any guarantee that I'd win big again, I also started buying lottery tickets. Not just in Pennsylvania, but because we lived on the New York State line, I would also buy tickets every day in New York. I used up our cash advance limits on credit cards and got new credit cards with more cash advance limits. When I would finally win something substantial at the casino, the only thing I could do with it was to try to pay down credit card bills while at the same time try to keep the utilities on and the mortgage paid. I was not only getting nowhere fast, but the panic and terror I was living had overtaken my life twenty-four hours a day. I would wake up in the middle of the night hundreds of times with the most horrible sense of dread and fear and wish that I would just die in my sleep.

I just kept making it worse. I used every dollar I could find trying to win enough money to replace what was missing, and just dug a deeper hole closer to hell.

And then the day came when I had to tell my husband. I knew I was doomed. I knew my life was going to get worse, but I had no idea how much worse. After work, I asked him to sit down with me to talk about something. He hated to talk, and he hated it when I asked him to talk to me. I told him that I was going to tell him "the worst thing you've ever heard in your life," then and proceeded to tell him that there should be a certain amount of money in the office trust account, and that there was nothing there. I was literally on my knees on the family room floor, begging him to forgive me, telling him I thought I could fix it, and that I had made it so much worse.

At first, he looked like he thought I was joking, and then he looked like he was going to kill me. I was sobbing and tried to tell him what had happened, and he just kept asking me how I could be so stupid. I told him I had tried to borrow the money from my relatives but couldn't.

After about half an hour of me sobbing and him pacing, he told me he was going to call his father and ask him to help. I had a really bad feeling, because his father was not a nice person, didn't like anyone much, and never thought I was good enough for his son because I'd been married before and had children. He always thought his son should end up with some wealthy socialite since he was a lawyer.

My husband went to the bedroom to make his call and came back about half an hour later. I was still sitting on the floor, still sobbing. I prayed that he'd have something hopeful to tell me, like his dad said he'd help him out, give him his inheritance early, or something fantastic like that. (Definition of *fantastic*: fantasy world stuff).

My husband's face was red, and he was seething. He said, "My father said he'd help me on one condition. He said I'd have to slit your throat first."

That day began my real descent into hell on earth. My home devolved into something akin to an insane asylum. That's exactly how it felt. Now there was really no way out for me. There wasn't going to be any escape from the addictions and sicknesses, and there wasn't going to be any hope for me to have a new life away from him.

My home became a place filled with rage, day and night. Terror, day and night. Threats and four-letter words. My husband told me that *no one* could ever know what had happened—not because he wanted to protect *me* but because he wasn't going to let me ruin *his* career. He said he was going to try to think of some way to fix it, and in the meantime, he was going to punish me. He often told me I would never have a nickel unless I crawled to him on my hands and knees, begging for it.

He regularly told me that, if anyone ever found out what had happened, he would make sure I would spend the rest of my life in prison. I would get up in the morning, take care of all our rescues, inside and outside, fix breakfast, work in the office all day and then come home to fix dinner. After dinner, I would clean the house for two or three hours, and he would sit in the living room in front of the TV, watching the most violent programs he could find, shuffling sports cards in huge piles on the coffee table, writing numbers on tablets of paper, eating junk food, screaming at me or threatening me.

I was in agony every day, and there wasn't a damn thing I could do to make anything better. I told him a million times I was sorry, and it seemed that he was truly, sickeningly happy that he had something so bad to hold against me. I had always been good to him, had never cheated on him, and pretty much did everything for him. He was a pretty lousy husband, and he knew it, and since we'd been battling over his addictions for so many years, he now had something that he could hold up to me and tell me to shut up if I ever thought about complaining about anything he did, ever again. Not only did he tell me he never wanted to hear anything again about how much I didn't like something he did, but he would always remind me, "I will make sure you spent the rest of your life in prison." His favorite line for more than a year.

Christmas Day 2005

On Christmas Day 2005, I found a Post-it note on the couch with a phone number and an e-mail address obviously written by a female. He would later admit that he had been "pursuing" a young female law clerk—twenty-eight years young—at the courthouse, and that they had talked often about going to concerts together and spending time together. I was fifty-four at the time, and she was younger than my daughters. To say that I was heartsick wasn't the half of it. I had a strong suspicion that this young female law clerk probably wasn't that interested in my overweight, overstressed husband, but in his mind, she wanted him. He would later tell me that it was *my* fault that he hadn't continued to pursue her and found happiness for himself. "If it wasn't for you, I could have been happy!"

~ ~ ~

I have attached a copy of one page from my husband's online "recovery" journal, which he posted on December 27, 2005.

I believed his intentions were good.

And I also remember my mother teaching me when I was just a child, "The road to hell is paved with good intentions."

And it was.

General » Recovery Journals » **My first day of sobriety**
http://lightwave.proboards48.com/index.cgi?board=journal&action=display&thread=1135740635

My first day of sobriety
Post by rpl on Dec 27, 2005, 10:30pm

I have been p/mb free for approximately 31 hours. After being in denial for almost 40 years, sadly it has taken me to age 52 to finally admit I have an addiction and that I am powerless over it. I believe that God led me to find this site and reading the posts has given me the desire to really want to commit to being sober and p/mb free. I've been with the same woman for 19 years and she knows I have this addiction. It has totally destroyed my marriage and any sense of intimacy I have with her. I told her I was finally prepared to admit to and confess my addiction and seek help. She is entirely skeptical since I made many promises in the past. The difference know is that I believe God is allowing me to begin to empathize with and understand some of the pain I have caused her. After 19 years of her trying to deal with this she has every right to doubt me and walk away.
Anybody who reads this post should listen to somebody who knows: P/Mb is a sickness that will destroy your life. If you are a young person dabbling in it, DONT! You wont begin to know the price you will pay in your life and in your relationships if you let yourself be deceived into believing it's harmless.
I read many of the great posts of the senior members and highly recommend them to new members. Here's my initial action plan.
1. Fully admit my addiction and confess powerless over it.
2. Seek out God's help and forgiveness.
3. Invest in prayer and God's word.
4. Fully destroy and rid myself of any trace of P
5. Full accountability to my wife of my actions.
6. Abstain from any MB
7. Understand and eliminate my triggers: Movies, television shows pictures and articles that are sexually suggestive.
8. TALK to my wife about my feelings.
9. Actively participate in this board and be accountable to all here.
10. Study and read up on my addiction and make every effort to understand.
11. Fill up spare time with productive, healthy choices.
12. Support others struggling with this addiction.
13. Work harder at developing empathy for my wife and try to fully understand the pain this has caused her.
Unfortunately, I live in a rural area where I can't find a trained addiction counselor nor any SAA groups. I'll take all the prayer and suggestions anyone wants to offer me. Regards, RPL

Re: My first day of sobriety
Post by gottabealthis on Dec 28, 2005, 6:15am

Congratulations rpl and that plan looks like a winner! I am gonna steal some of it and use it in my plan.

Gottabealthis

Re: My first day of sobriety
Post by tiktok on Dec 28, 2005, 2:39pm

This looks like a good plan, rpl! And from what I've read here in the last few weeks and from my own experience, having a plan is a very important step in overcoming this addiction. Good luck!

Re: My first day of sobriety
Post by imaj76 on Dec 29, 2005, 12:24am

Congratulations!

"Do not be afraid or discouraged. Be determined and
confident. For I will be with you wherever you go."

Joshua 1:9

This verse has kept me going during hard times.
Remember we are saved by Grace. Look up to HIM more than the addiction
is what I learned in my walk of faith. As you draw near to God HIS
desires become yours purging away anything that is not of HIM.

God Bless!

L

Re: My first day of sobriety
Post by witness on Dec 29, 2005, 5:26am

EXCERPTS FROM HIS ADDICTIONS JOURNAL (4

http://lightwave.proboards48.com/index.cgi?board=journal&action=print&thread... 12/17/2007

Do not ever let anyone convince you that pornography, masturbation, and sex addictions are normal, or that "everyone does it."

That is a lie from the pit of hell.

The most excellent, reasoned, and sensible explanation of P/M/S addictions I've ever come across is this:

When the human brain is exposed to stimulation, as most of us know well, there are chemicals that are released in the body that give us certain "feelings." Not unlike a runner who gets an endorphin rush, someone who is sexually stimulated also gets an intense "rush."

Information from Wikipedia and other online resources reveals that the hormone dopamine is a neurotransmitter that helps control the brain's reward and pleasure centers. There are distinctly different dopamine systems, and one system specifically plays a major role in reward-motivated behavior.

Not unlike an alcoholic or a drug addict, the rush from repeated stimulation starts to wane over time. A tolerance is built up. It takes more and more booze, or drugs, or sexual stimulation to elicit the same intoxicating feelings you once got from "just a little". This explanation that makes so much sense to me explains there is an area in the brain that controls reasoning, and the chemicals being released in the body are constantly washing over the brain, making you feel high, stimulated, excited, whatever words you choose to describe your own "rush." You need more and more stimulation, sometimes over a period of weeks or months, sometimes over a period of years, until you get no, or almost no, rush from what was once such an intoxicating feeling.

At the same time, the area of your brain that controls judgment and reasoning, the cerebrum, literally starts to erode after incessant, constant, excessive bombardment with these nifty chemicals.

This makes so much sense to me! I have seen so many people who once seemed so rational and reasonable and sensible turn into complete idiots, or abusers, or total wasted lives, after spending years "indulging" themselves in whatever their "rush" of choice might be.

In the case of P/M/S addictions, I will always believe they can be much more dangerous and deadly than even drug or alcohol addictions. The sexual addictions and rushes are just so much more powerful, and it becomes so much more difficult to maintain or recreate the initial rush that so many people resort to perversions that most of us will never, ever understand. When I was reading posts from other addicts on my husband's recovery journal website I learned the most disgusting and perverted things I'd ever heard, including one young man who carried disposable baby diapers in his duffel bag so he could masturbate into them, and then eventually started thinking about a baby being in the diaper in his fantasies.

Of course you don't want to hear that. Neither did I.

But ignorance is not bliss!

Christmas 2006

The Christmas holidays had always been my very favorite time of the year since I was a small child. When I had children of my own, I did everything I could think of to make it special for my own kids, and when I had grandchildren it was even better. I would do my best to make sure that everyone got their biggest wishes and dreams fulfilled on Christmas morning, and loved nothing more than watching them open gifts that they never expected to get. I did the same for my daughters and their husbands. I always wanted to know what their biggest wish-list items were by talking to their spouses, and would move heaven and earth to be able to get it for them. That often meant lots of credit card debt and putting off paying bills for a month, but it was *so* worth it.

But by Christmastime in 2006, my home had already been a 24-hour-a-day nightmare for many, many months. Insanity. Grief. Anguish. I couldn't fix anything, and I couldn't escape. In 2006, there was no Thanksgiving celebration with family, and there was no Christmas celebration with anyone. There were no lights and decorations, there was no tree, there was no Christmas music, there were no friends and family. There was, day after day and night after night, my husband seething, cursing, threatening, watching the most violent movies he could find, looking at porn, shuffling sports cards, overeating, sleeping in the guest room.

It was Christmas Eve, and my house was dark and very empty. I was literally curled up in a fetal position on the couch in the family room, sobbing and aching with so much heartache I can't begin to describe it. Christmas Eve was always my most favorite day, so much better than Christmas Day. And it was just slipping away in this insanity and darkness. My husband walked by me to go into the bathroom, and he stopped long enough to look down at me. He started smirking and chuckling and said "You have got to be the most pathetic thing I have ever seen in my life! You make me sick! Why don't you just have another pity party for yourself somewhere else?"

I just doubled over even more, in so much pain, in uncontrollable pain. I could never, ever get this day back. I could never, ever get back the time I'd wasted in my life with this sick man. It was just such overwhelming grief and sadness and emptiness.

~ ~ ~

Within a week of Christmas in 2006, I got a call from my daughter saying that my husband had suffered a heart attack. He was taken to the hospital in an ambulance from his office, and his heart had stopped in the emergency room. His doctor had given him a clot-busting drug, sending him off to a hospital in Erie by Life Flight helicopter. When I met my daughter at the hospital, I just doubled over with grief. I didn't want him to die, but I did. I didn't know what to feel, or think, or do.

I asked a friend to go with me to the hospital, two hours away, late at night, and prayed all the way there that he would survive. I was terrified that I'd get there and be told that he had died; and for some reason, I was sure that if he was given another chance, things would be different. I was sure.

When I saw him in the CCU, all hooked up to wires and monitors and tubes, I didn't know what to say. He told me he believed he was being given another chance. He said "things are going to be different." I wanted so much to believe that, and so for a few days, I did.

He was thankful for being alive and was really different for a short time. And then the madness and seething came back, with a vengeance. While he was still in the hospital, having survived a stent procedure that repaired a 99 percent blockage in a coronary artery, the madness came back. What a miracle he'd been given, and all he could say was that he wished he had died.

While he was still home recuperating, just days after his stent procedure, the county informed him that they were taking away one of his two salaried positions because they felt he was overworked. The loss of nearly $30,000 in salary was the last thing we needed to hear. He became even angrier and more despondent, and even vengeful. Now he felt that everyone on earth was trying to destroy him, and since he couldn't take it out on the rest of *them*, he took it out on me even more than he already was.

When he finally went back to work, he was taking nearly a dozen different medications and hormones and his behavior became more and more bizarre. Several times he would take money that clients had just paid for retainers and tell me to take it to the casino, that I'd "better come back with some big money." One afternoon, he had my daughter cash a check for him for $1,000 and then told me he was taking me to the casino to "win big." I told him we needed too many things at home, and that I wanted to go to the grocery store. He just snarled at me and said we were going to go the casino, and I was going to win some money. He then stood over me for about two hours while I sat at a slot machine, until about $400 was gone, and I told him I wasn't going to stay any longer, and went to the car. He seethed all the way home.

October 2007

Nonstop insanity, nonstop grief, nonstop terror. My husband was in a constant state of rage, and I couldn't get out. I couldn't get away from it. I would do everything I could possibly think of to stay away from my house because it was sheer torture for me to be home. No matter how long I was able to stay away, I would always have to go back by the end of the day because my animals needed to be taken care of. They needed food and fresh water, and the litter boxes needed cleaning. There was always housework and laundry.

If I didn't go home to do it, absolutely nothing would get done. I know, because a few times I tried to stay away until very late, hoping he'd be asleep when I got home, thinking there was no way he would let our animals go hungry. But he did, many times. I would walk through the door to find the house a disaster and my rescues crying for food and water while my husband sat in front of the television with his sports cards and violence. He would just scream at me and torment me, sometimes literally for hours, often late into the night.

There were many times that I would be on my hands and knees cleaning the floors or scooping litter boxes, and he would stand over me and start calling me all kinds of filthy names, which had become routine for him, while I sobbed and begged him to leave me alone. Several times he would walk to the kitchen drawer where I kept the knives and would pull out the biggest one, a butcher knife. Twice he came at me saying he was trying to give it to me, and twice he slid it across the floor at me, telling me to do myself a favor and kill myself. He would say, "Put an end to your misery, will you, so you can put an end to my misery too?"

After one particularly terrifying weekend, I went to our office and faxed a two-page letter to Dr. Bazzoui, our psychiatrist and his friend, who had been "treating" him for years for depression. Instead of focusing on my husband's problems, they would invariably talk about cases and clients they had in common, either through Children and Youth

Services or the Public Defender's Office. After he had an appointment, I would ask him if he felt better talking to Dr. B., and he would always say "Not really," telling me they didn't usually talk about *his* problems—they talked about everyone else's problems.

In my letter to Dr. B., I begged him to help me. I wrote, "He has been threatening to kill me, himself, or both of us," and I told him my husband had said one of us wasn't going to survive the weekend. The weekends were always the worst. I begged Dr. B. to please get him admitted to some kind of treatment facility, or "*Please* do something!"

Dr. B.'s secretary did contact my husband and asked him to come in for an appointment. My husband came home from Dr. B's office after only a short time, and he had a plastic bag full of pill samples. He said Dr. B. had told him he wasn't taking enough medication, and he wanted him to start taking more. Dr. B. had known for quite some time about his addictions, the missing money from his trust account, and his violent behavior.

We had another battle, and he told me he was going to kill himself with the new pills and took six while he sat in front of me, counting them out one by one as he swallowed them, chuckling and grinning. I called the police for help, and he was taken to the hospital, where he stayed in the psychiatric ward for three days. He got no help; he told them that his wife was his only problem, and no one seemed to think he had a legitimate illness. He came home worse.

~ ~ ~

The last time I had an appointment with Dr. B. for my medication checkup—he had been writing my prescription for Paxil for years, and I had to see him three times a year to get refills—I blew up at him after trying to get him to help me with my husband's porn addiction. It had gotten so much worse and so out of control that I was more and more afraid of what he was going to do.

I told him I had not only found magazines, but one afternoon, while I was cleaning bookshelves in our basement, I picked up some magazine organizers to clean the shelving, and about a dozen magazines fell onto the floor. As I was picking them up, a lot of small pieces of magazine pages fell out of some *Sports Illustrated* magazines—not the swimsuit editions, just the regular sports-themed issues. My husband had clipped pictures from porn magazines and hidden them inside the pages of sports magazines.

All over the floor were small clippings of female body parts. Not naked female bodies but, rather, body parts, like women's legs spread without the rest of their bodies. Women's breasts without the rest of their bodies. There weren't women's faces; they were just body parts. I was sick to my stomach again. Why in the hell would someone want to look at body parts with no person attached to them?

What the hell kind of hobby is this?

I was trying to tell Dr. B. how distressing and frightening this was to me, and he said one of the most idiotic, stupid and uninformed things I've ever heard coming from any medical professional.

"I'm sure your husband's problem is just that he's having trouble getting an erection. His job is so stressful, and he probably feels bad that he can't maintain an erection, so he needs lots of help. I think all he really needs is some Viagra."

What? What did you just say?

I jumped up from my chair and started screaming at him. I told him he had no idea what pornography and masturbation addictions were, and that he'd damn well better go back to school before he ever tells anyone else something that insane! I told him he was going to totally destroy what was left of any patients' relationships if he continued to give that kind of perverted advice.

How stupid can a medical doctor, *a psychiatrist*, be? That's kind of like saying all the alcoholic really needs to deal with his alcohol addiction is a ride to the bar!

~ ~ ~

If things weren't already overwhelming and excruciatingly painful enough, I got a call from my oldest daughter early one morning while my husband was still in the psychiatric ward. I could not believe what she was telling me. *Her* husband was in the psychiatric ward of another hospital after swallowing two bottles of pills in front of her and their two boys the night before!

I was not going to ask myself, or ask God, "What else can go wrong?" because I knew that it could surely get worse. I just had this absolutely all-consuming feeling of dread and terror. It was as though my whole world was crashing in on me from every direction.

My youngest daughter had just told me she was pregnant after going through almost a year of IVF treatments, and I knew her husband was not only a cheater but could also be abusive. I was so afraid and in pain for her, and she didn't want me interfering in anything. Her pregnancy was high-risk because of her age, and she had gone through it all to try to save her marriage and, hopefully, make her husband happy.

So both of my daughters were in crisis situations, my husband was threatening to kill me almost daily, and by now, I was regularly hyperventilating, never getting any restful sleep, suffering from panic attacks, and trying to deal with restless legs syndrome most nights, sometimes jumping from bed screaming, trying desperately to walk it off. I still had so much work to do and animals to care for every single day, and there was absolutely nowhere I could go for help.

October 22, 2007

On October 22, my husband and I had a knock-down, drag-out fight in our office after he started screaming at my daughter. I told her to go home, and he told me it was going to be my last day of freedom. He picked up the phone, and I heard him telling someone that he had "just discovered" that I had stolen money from his trust account, and that he wanted me to be prosecuted. I started screaming and took the phone away from him. He started laughing at me and told me he was going to "see to it you spend the rest of your life in prison," like he had been saying for months. This time he had made a call, and he was actually going to try to do it.

I just remember begging him, "Please, don't do this! What will happen to our animals?" And he just glared at me, saying he'd either "get rid of them all or have them euthanized." I could take him threatening to harm me a million times, but I could never, ever stand anyone threatening those animals. I just ran at him and started hitting him in the face, and he, in turn, knocked me from one end of the office to the other. I picked up a small office chair and threw it in his direction, but I missed him. He slammed me up against the walls, knocking me down to the floor several times. I just kept begging him not to let anything happen to them, and his eyes were just wild, his countenance terrifying. I grabbed my purse and keys and ran out the door, trying to gather what was left of my mind and trying to think of how I'd get the animals away from him.

But I couldn't! There were too many! There was no place for me to take them! And I couldn't leave them! What in the hell was I going to do?

I went home and wasn't there more than half an hour before I didn't have to make any decisions for myself. A police officer came walking up the driveway and wanted to talk to me. My husband wanted to file charges against me for assault.

~ ~ ~

I went to the city police station and met with Officer Mike Ward. Mike told me that he was going to add the charge of harassment to the simple assault charge because, as he said, it might "help" me in the long run. He told me that the police usually did that because if there was a lesser charge than simple assault, the district attorney would typically agree to let the defendant plead to the lesser charge. He assured me that pleading to the lesser charge of harassment was going to be much better for me than having to plead guilty to simple assault.

After getting details from me about my side of the story, Mike Ward asked me if I would like to file assault or other charges against my husband. He told me I had every right to file charges as well. I didn't have to think for more than a second about it. There was no way in hell I was going to file any charges against my husband. If I filed charges against him, it was going to be in the newspaper, and then it was going to go to the Disciplinary Board. I was sure he'd lose his county position, and I was sure he would be facing suspension if he was charged criminally. I just could not risk that. If my husband lost his job with the county as chief public defender, we would never survive financially, and I would inevitably lose my home and my rescues.

Mike also asked me questions about my husband's allegations that I had taken money from his trust account, and I heard myself telling him that whatever my husband told him was true. I told him my husband had known for more than a year about the money and that my home had become a nightmare of epic proportions since the day I told him. Mike told me that he would eventually have to file charges against me for taking the money, and I told him I understood. He said it would probably be awhile because they always had to do investigations before filing charges. Mike would later tell me that they were investigating three other people in the county in similar situations for taking money from their employers, but that really didn't make me feel any better.

So in answer to his question about whether or not I wanted to file my own charges, I just told Mike Ward no and did not.

I've already told you I was a genius.

~ ~ ~

I had also told Mike Ward that I couldn't take living with my husband's addictions anymore. Mike's eyes got really big, and he looked as though he thought I was going to give him some big drug bust or something juicy. He had pulled me aside, and he said, "You said your husband has addictions? What kind of addictions? Drugs?"

I said, "No, not drugs, he's a porn addict."

Poor Mike, he looked as though I'd just stolen his Christmas gifts from under his tree. He just said, "Oh." and never asked me another question about it. I knew he was disappointed, but it wasn't until much later I would find out why he was more than ambivalent about my husband's porn obsession.

It eventually became public that Mike Ward had been investigated by the police department for looking at pornography on police computers while on duty.

Hey, everybody does it! Right, Mike?

~ ~ ~

On October 22, district magistrate Dom Cercone arraigned me and released me on $5,000 ROR bail. I was released on my own recognizance conditioned on the restriction that I have no contact with my husband. I assumed that didn't matter, because I also assumed my husband would eventually drop the charges and contact me and we would somehow work it out. He hadn't been able to do much of anything for himself since I'd known him, and since he no longer had his mother either, I assumed he'd get desperate and want to "fix" things.

Domestic Relations

THE NEXT DAY I filed an emergency petition for spousal support because I knew it was possible that my husband would not give me anything voluntarily. I really thought I knew the process well because I'd spent nearly twenty years helping my husband file complaints and petitions with the court system, and it was pretty much always the same.

Looking back, I honestly should have known better. Nothing was ever going to be pretty much the same for me regardless of what I tried to do in the court system. My husband was part of that court system.

I drove to the county courthouse and went upstairs to the Domestic Relations offices. They had installed security doors and intercoms since the last time I was there, and I had to wait in a small waiting area at the top of the stairs. I buzzed for an employee and told her what I needed. I asked how I could file an emergency petition for spousal support since I not only had no money, but I had just lost my only source of income.

When I asked her what the specific procedures were for filing an emergency petition, she told me she wasn't aware of any. I figured either she was new and didn't know the process, or she was lying.

She gave me forms to fill out to file a *pro se* petition and to ask the court that the filing fee be waived. She left me at the top of the stairs with my forms and a pen, and I didn't see her again for about half an hour. While I was filling out my forms, my cell phone rang. I looked at it and saw that it was my husband. I honestly didn't know what to do. I had been told by Cercone that if I attempted to contact my husband for anything, he would have me put in jail.

I answered the phone. My husband said, "Where are you?" And I said, "I'm at the courthouse." He said, "What are you doing *there*?" I told him I had been told I wasn't allowed to talk to him, and that he'd better not call me again. He was very angry, but I wasn't sure exactly why he was calling me.

I did not find out until months later–from my husband– that someone from the Domestic Relations Office had called him to tell him I was there wanting to file a petition for spousal support. He had called me while I was sitting there because they had *told* him I was sitting there.

I had gone to the courthouse as a private citizen expecting to be able to make use of the court system just as any other citizen of the county would expect to do. What I didn't realize at the time was that "the fix" was already in. I was never, *ever*, going to have a chance at anything equitable or fair in the McKean County court system.

When I got back to town, I called Cercone's office and asked to speak to him. I asked him why it was all right for my husband to be contacting me but that he (Cercone) had threatened me with jail if I contacted my husband. Cercone started to make some lame excuse and tried to tell me it wasn't the same thing, and I told him he had *no* idea who my husband was, or what he was capable of. I started to tell him that my husband often threatened to harm me, and that he had most recently been threatening me at home with a large kitchen knife.

Honest to God, I heard Dom Cercone start *laughing*, and I could tell he was holding the phone away from his ear and was playing to his crowd at his office. He was intentionally speaking extra loudly and, in a mocking tone of voice, said, "Ron Langella has been threatening you with *knives*? *Really*, Cathy?" And he laughed again.

I told him again that he had no idea who my husband really was, and he just told me I'd better do exactly what he, Cercone, had told me to do, or I'd be in more trouble.

November 2, 2007

It had been more than a week since the altercation in our office, and I was released on my own recognizance. I had applied for any benefits I might be able to get from the

Public Assistance Office. The laws in Pennsylvania would have clearly given me access to my own property, as well as much of our joint property, but I had no lawyer, no money, and my husband was a lawyer. There was no way I was going to be able to get anything—at least not right now.

I had made an appointment with the welfare office for the afternoon of November 2, and they had given me a list of information and documentation that I needed to take with me to the appointment so they could process my application. Everything I had, like tax returns or bank account statements, was in our office, in my desk or in the filing cabinets. My husband had changed the locks on the office door, even though the office building was in both our names, and there had not yet been any court proceedings determining anything.

I called my daughter while she was at home for lunch and told her what I needed. She told me that my husband was going to be out of town for the rest of the afternoon and wouldn't be back until the end of the day. She told me I could stop at the office around three o'clock to get things from my desk.

My daughter swore to me that she didn't set me up, but when I walked through the office door at ten minutes after three, my husband was standing over her, dictating something. He was not out of town, and it certainly wasn't the end of the day. He put his palm up to me, gesturing for me to stay back, and told me to wait until he was done dictating. After a few minutes, he walked to the back of the office.

I walked over to my desk, which was directly behind my daughter's desk, sat down, and started talking to her. I asked her why she was still there, and why she was still helping him. She started yelling at me, "What do you expect me to do? I need this job! I'm pregnant! No one else is going to hire me *now*!"

I started crying, she kept yelling, and all of a sudden I realized that my husband was in the back of the office with the phone to his ear.

I heard him say, "My wife is here at my office, in violation of her bail conditions, and she needs to go to jail!"

Literally within two minutes there were *four* police cars in front of or near our office. *Four!* I heard my husband tell a police officer that he wanted me arrested. He told them I had violated my bail conditions.

He was smiling at me.

I was escorted down Main Street with crowds of people standing around, and was told to get in the back of a police car. I was sobbing and kept trying to tell them that I had called ahead and that my daughter had told me to come by at three. By now, it wasn't yet three thirty, and I was already apparently in custody.

I was beyond panic-stricken. Again. I just kept trying to tell myself, they'll just give me a warning and let me go home. Screw the welfare office, I'll make do some other way! I'll tell them I have no way to access my own papers, and they'll understand, right?

Yeah, right.

I was taken first to the city police station and put in a holding cell. I had absolutely no idea how much worse it was going to get. I had been crying nonstop since I was at our office, and had picked up my Diet Coke that I had left over from lunch. I was terribly thirsty and started walking into the police station with it. Officer Mike Ward grabbed my drink from my hand and threw it in the garbage can. "You can't have that here, and I'm sick of your shit!" I heard him call Cercone's office, and he was apparently told to take me there. I was placed back in the police car, in handcuffs, and we went back to Cercone's.

There must have been other court proceedings going on, because when I first got there, I wasn't taken to the courtroom but instead was escorted into a small office with a desk and a couple of chairs. Dom Cercone walked down the hall several times past me, and several times stuck his head in the door to make comments to me. I asked him if I could make a phone call to my brother. I was going to ask him to post bail for me. He said I could.

I called my brother at his business and was sobbing, asking him to please come get me out so I could go home. He said he would "see what he could do," but he never came. Earlier in the week, I had stopped to see my brother to ask him if he could help me with groceries or anything at all. I had tried to tell him what had been going on with my husband, and I got less than a sympathetic ear from my brother. He had snickered at me when I told him about my husband's addictions, said something like "You've got to be kidding" when I started crying, and had then proceeded to tell me that my husband had already told him that I had taken money from his account because I was a gambling addict and was very sick.

About ten minutes later, while I was still sitting at the desk, still sobbing and very terrified, Cercone stuck his head back in the doorway and, with a big smile on his face, said, "Cathy, you know what I was just thinking? Your brother can't post bail for you! You've just *violated* your bail. I am *revoking* your bail!"

I wasn't just sobbing anymore, I was wailing. I started begging him, *"Please!* No! Please don't do this! I have sick animals I have to take care of! Please! No! I'm not a flight risk! I need to take care of my animals!"

And Dominic Cercone, still with a big smile on his face, said, "Cathy, I know all about your *fifty* cats! You'd better forget about them and start worrying about yourself!"

No! Please! No! Please, don't do this!

I told him I had one cat that was in renal failure and that she desperately needed to get her sub-q fluids every day after work. It was already late in the afternoon.

He just smiled again and walked away.

I was handcuffed again and placed in the back seat of Officer Linda Close's police car, where I sobbed and screamed until we reached the county jail, praying God would somehow get me back home. I was so terrified for my rescues. It was already dark, and I knew Jody desperately needed her fluids to stay alive.

Booking

I REMEMBER THE police car pulling into a garage and a garage door closing behind us. I honestly wasn't sure where I was. The door opened, and I was told to get out. I vaguely remember Linda leading me through a door to the booking room. I remember a big desk, some filing cabinets, a couple of wooden chairs, lots of big doors, and a big cell that seemed to be part of the room. I knew I was in shock. My head was pounding so fiercely I was sure I was going to have a stroke. But then again, my heart was pounding so fast, and I was so dizzy, I thought maybe I'd have a heart attack. I knew that either my head or my heart was just going to explode. The lights in the room were really bright, and my eyes could hardly focus. Everything seemed to be spinning around me.

This can't be real. This is some horrendous nightmare. This has to be some kind of sick joke. Oh my God! This has to be hell! It's hell, isn't it? I really died, and I went straight to hell!

A female corrections officer was talking to me. Short, thin, young blonde-haired girl, who seemed vaguely familiar, but I had no reason to know who she was. Or did I? She was giving me orders. She was giving me things. She gave me some bright orange clothing and a towel.

No! This can't be real! I have to get home! Jody needs her fluids! It's past time to give Jody her fluids! Someone is going to come for me! Someone is going to call for me! Someone is going to say they made a mistake and I'm not supposed to be here! Jody would get so sick so fast if she missed her fluids!

The thin blonde girl took me to an adjacent room and told me to take off all of my clothes. I was wailing. "*Why?*" She told me it was "rules". "No! Please, no!" She stood and watched while I took off every single piece of clothing I was wearing. I was beyond humiliated. Head throbbing, room spinning, chest ready to explode. I had to stand facing her, totally naked. She picked up a plastic squirt bottle and started spraying me with it, head to toe. I was sobbing, screaming! "Please, no!" She told me to turn around. I turned around, and she squirted me again, head to toe, with the cold liquid from the plastic squirt bottle. I asked her why. I asked her what it was. "Lice killer." *Oh my God! God! Where are you? Why have you left me?*

She handed me the towel and told me to take a shower, to wash it off. She stood outside the shower while I tried to rinse it off. Stabbing head pain, room spinning more, total desperation, total panic, total fear! *God! Please, help me! Please!* But I was sure God wasn't helping me. I was sure he had left me.

Then I remembered where I had seen the young blonde corrections officer. She was a client of my husband's, and I had seen her in our office.

~ ~ ~

I tried to dry off, but my hair was now soaking wet, and I only had one small towel. I was given orange pants and an orange shirt to put on, and was told to sit in the wooden chair next to the desk. There were people in and out of the room, mostly men. I guess mostly corrections officers. It seemed to be evening, but I honestly wasn't sure. The jail employees were all talking and laughing and joking around me. Talking about other things. There were other guys that were inmates, all dressed in orange, with a lot of tattoos and long hair.

I was told that they had to empty my purse, which they had already taken from me, and that it had to be inventoried. The blonde girl took a sheet of paper and started writing everything that she took out. She took my prescription medications and started to write them down. I said I had to have them, that they were blood pressure medications, she couldn't take them from me. "Don't worry," I was told. "You'll get them if you need them." They inventoried every piece of anything that was in my purse and went through my wallet. I think I had three $20 bills, and I was told that it would go into my "account," and I could use it later.

I thought, *What do you mean, my account? I'm not staying here! I'm going home! I have animals that are really sick! I have a little girl that is in renal failure! I'm not staying here! I don't need an account! I hit my husband, but he hit me too! He knocked me around the room! He threatened me, he threatened my rescues! He has been abusing and threatening me for years! This is a sick joke! This is a freaking mistake! This is not right!*

I was sobbing again, really feeling as though my body was just going to give out. I kept telling them my head hurt so bad! "Please, I need something for my head!" I was told I could ask for something "later."

~ ~ ~

I told the blonde girl, my husband's client, that I was terrified for my animals, and tried to explain to her that I had critically ill rescues that needed constant care. She gave me a piece of notebook paper and asked me if I would like to write down the names and phone numbers of people that might be able to help me with them. I tried to clear my head enough to remember phone numbers, but I could barely remember names. I wrote down the name of my best friend of forty years but couldn't remember her phone number. I wrote down a friend that used to be assistant manager of the local SPCA and had also done pet-sitting for me when we had gone on vacation a few years before. I couldn't remember her number either, so I wrote down what I thought it might be. I wrote down my oldest daughter's name and number, and the name and number of the mayor's wife, with whom I'd had many conversations about her own rescue attempts. Her father was a huge animal lover as well, and I had talked with him several times about my rescues in his daughter's restaurant. I was sure they would help. Somehow.

I then wrote down the names of the sickest of my cats. *Jody.* She was in renal failure, and because I had treated other cats in renal failure and given them extended quality of life, I had been giving her daily subcutaneous fluids that were keeping her going, keeping her comfortable and happy. I would check her regularly to make sure she wasn't getting dehydrated and, if she appeared to be, I would give her fluids more than once a day. Long before Jody got sick, I'd bought an IV pole and always kept boxes of needles, Venosets and cases of lactated ringers. I had learned that fluids were often a wonderful way to get them through other illnesses, and could make a huge difference, especially if they had a tendency to become dehydrated.

I wrote down *Jeter* and *Johnny D.* They were both very small feral kitten rescues. They were sisters and were both very sick. I made up jugs of kitten formula from condensed milk and other ingredients from a recipe I got from our vet and gave them Nutri-Cal and eye drops and anything else I thought would help.

I wrote down *Spinnerboy*, who came into our house after living months outside, often spending his nights in our heated shed in the backyard. I had learned that he had been cared for by a well-to-do woman who lived a few doors down from me, and as well-intentioned as she was, I don't think she realized that she was causing a crisis for Spinnerboy when she went to Florida for the winters. When he came down with a really bad skin infection, I took him to the vet and got him pills that he had to take twice a day, and he was just the most well-behaved boy you could ever meet. He would look at me as though he knew exactly what I had for him, and that it made him feel better, and he would let me pop his pill down his throat without giving me any trouble.

I wrote out the details of the animals that needed the most urgent treatment and handed the paper back to the blonde girl, who said she would "take care of it."

I don't know what she meant, but no one ever helped me. I don't know if anyone was ever called, or if anyone was ever contacted.

Following is a copy of the notebook paper notes I wrote out, begging for help, that obviously didn't go to anyone, because I was given the original back when I was released from jail.

360-8698
3620393 Janel Riel (Tom Riel's wife) Tom said
she would help many times before - # in phone book

Please ask if they could get volunteers to
help me!!!

Cherri Nichols (David)   362-2713
159 South Avenue Bradford   (don't remember
                              her phone #)
(she is my oldest & best friend - also has animals)
                          (maybe cell 366-0266)

Becky Gonzales (Rob)   (366-1481)
Minard Run Road   (don't remember her
                        phone #)

(long time animal lover - was SPCA mgr.
                and Dr. MacNeil's tech)
she has also been my pet-sitter many times

                        Kim Thompson
                        225-3124

_____

"JODY" - BLACK & WHITE, VERY THIN, IN RENAL
           FAILURE, HIDES BEHIND TV IN CABINET
           IN FAMILY ROOM - SHE NEED 50-100 cc
           LACTATED RINGERS AT LEAST ONCE A DAY.
    TUBES OF NUTRICAL IN KITCHEN DRAWER (END)
        NEEDLES IN SAME DRAWER

"SPINNERBOY"   GRAY TIGER, LOSING MOST FUR ON
                HIND QUARTERS - HAS PILLS IN ALUM
    "CLAVAMOX" STRIPS IN SAME DRAWER - NEEDS 2 A DAY

"JOHNNY D" - BABY TIGER (JETER'S BROTHER)
        NEEDS HEATED FORMULA (ROOM TEMP
                                    AT LEAST)
        AND NUTRICAL
        EYE DROPS IN SAME DRAWER

"JETER" - BABY BROWN/GRAY TIGER -
NEEDS HIS FORMULA EVERY EVENING
IN DROPPER ON COUNTER TOP. HE
STANDS ON REAR LEGS TO DRINK.

FORMULA IS IN TUBS EITHER IN KITCHEN OR
SHELVES WHERE CAT FOOD IS. MIX 1:2 -
1 PART POWDER, 2 PARTS WATER. PUT IN
EMPTY CONTAINER & SHAKE WELL TO MIX

Please Ron needs to get cat litter, litter box
liners, paper plates, Reynolds wrappers.
Canned cat food, bagged cat food, paper towels
(at least 16 rolls) and spray cleaner (at least 4)
Kitten milk replacement formula (walmart)
in tub (powdered)

~ ~ ~

Before I was taken to the women's cell block, I was told that they thought it might be a good idea if I talked to a counselor. Maybe I was having trouble dealing with everything and I needed someone to talk to? That is when I met Beth.

I was taken into a separate room with a big table and some chairs and a locked door and was introduced to Beth. She seemed to be about my age, was very pretty, very soft-spoken, and very kind to me. She sat across the table from me and told me that she had been called in because she was told I was having trouble dealing with everything.

I started telling her what had happened earlier in the day and how I ended up in jail. I told her I had begged Cercone to let me go home to take care of my animals, and how he had laughed at me. I told her how worried and scared I was that no one would be taking care of them, and that Jody had to have her fluids every day, or she would die.

Beth told me that she knew some things about me. She said she knew my husband from her work at the jail, that she would see him occasionally, but that she didn't know him personally. She also told me she knew that I cared for rescues. She had followed the articles in the *Era* when I tried to fight City Hall, and they had held hearings over the rescues I was caring for outdoors.

After about twenty minutes, Beth told me that she wanted to warn me about someone I was going to meet in the women's cell block. She wanted to prepare me for something she was concerned I would be upset about.

What else could there be? I was already in hell, so who was I going to meet that would be worse?

Beth asked me if I had seen the stories in the *Era* about the woman that was accused of leaving her Great Danes to starve to death at her home in Bradford. Of course I had. Everyone everywhere knew about that horrific story. "Well," she said, "her name is Cheryl, and she's in the cell block, so you are going to meet her." Beth said she knew I loved animals, and she was concerned that I might be upset being around Cheryl.

Of course I had heard the stories about Cheryl. I just hadn't remembered her name. I knew the stories about Cheryl, and many more stories about Cheryl, because my husband was Cheryl's lawyer! I remembered well my husband going to see Cheryl at the jail sometime ago, and I remembered well my husband telling me that he was sure Cheryl was guilty, and that he was also sure that Cheryl was crazy!

"But," she told me, "I want you to know"—and she looked straight into my eyes, across that table—"she didn't do what they said she did! I *know* she didn't do it!" She told me that Cheryl's dogs had not died at her hands, and that the truth would eventually come out, she was sure of that. She told me that she really loved Cheryl, and she knew she wasn't capable of doing anything that awful, and that she wanted me to know that Cheryl wasn't who they were saying she was. She wanted me to please try to meet Cheryl with an open mind.

Meeting Cheryl was the last thing I was worried about. Honest to God.

~ ~ ~

I was eventually led down what seemed like a very long hallway with lots of closed doors on either side. At the end of the hallway was a door to the left with a big window in the upper half. I think it was Brandy, the corrections officer and my husband's client, who took me through that door. It seemed filled to overflowing with females of all ages. I immediately noticed that the room was very small for so many people—I'd guess about fifteen by twenty feet—with several doors off the room on three sides. There were three round steel tables bolted to the cement floor and four small steel stools around each table, also bolted to the floor. There was a small TV bolted high up on one of the walls, a small bookshelf, and several mattresses on the floor. Women—some were very young-looking girls—were sitting on stools, sitting on mattresses on the floor. Some were watching TV, some were reading, some were huddled in conversation.

No one really seemed to notice me, which I thought was really strange. I was so beyond despairing by then, and my face was swollen and beet-red. I had been sobbing for hours. I was so sick to my stomach, and my head was pounding. But no one came to console me or ask me how I was or what was wrong or anything like that, which I thought was bizarre. The thoughts raced through my head again, *Am I in hell? Did I die today and this is where I ended up?*

I remember being told that there were no beds for me, that the jail was overcrowded. Someone said they'd have to get me a mattress and sheets. I sat on one of the steel stools until they found a mattress for me and put it on the floor between two doorways. I soon learned that most of the "doorways" off that small room were cells, and the "doors" were made of steel bars. One open doorway had a curtain across the opening and was a shower room. One of the girls came over, very matter-of-factly, and put a sheet on my mattress and a pillowcase on a small pillow. She asked me if I'd brought anything with me, like socks or underwear, and when I said I hadn't, she went to her cell and came back with a pair of white socks, which she handed me.

I have never forgotten that. If I was in hell, would someone do something nice for me and give me a pair of their socks? I didn't think so.

I lay down on my mattress on the floor and sobbed. I would soon find out that seeing someone crying, or even hysterically wailing, was so commonplace in that small room that most of the other girls never even reacted or seemed to notice. And most of them honestly didn't care.

They all had their own problems, and they certainly weren't going to make *you* another one.

My mind was racing, and the terror again washed over me. Jody should have had her fluids by now. She could not go more than a day without her fluids without going downhill fast. It was nighttime, and the cats should have already had their dinner. Who was taking care of them? Who was giving Jody her sub-q fluids? Who was changing litter boxes or cleaning up after them? I had done it alone for so long, and I was trying to imagine who might be taking care of them.

Then I tried to comfort myself. *It's Friday night*, I thought. *By tomorrow morning, someone will have come to get me out of here, and I'll go home and take care of my animals like I've done every single day for years. Yeah, that's what will happen. One of my daughters, or one of my friends, or even my husband, will be so worried about me, and about the cats, and they'll do whatever it takes to get me out of here. My husband will wake up tomorrow and feel good that he taught me a lesson, and he won't want to do any of the work himself, so he'll come and get me. He'll tell me I deserved to be terrified, and how I was a horrible, terrible, waste of a person, and that he hoped I would believe him now.*

Remember when he kept telling me that he would see to it I spent the rest of my life in prison and I would always scream and cry and beg him not to take me away from the animals that needed me? He would come get me and tell me that it was just a taste of what he could do to me if he wanted to, and how lucky I was that he rescued me. He would remind me that I would have nothing without him, and that he was lowering himself to do something for me.

That's okay. I'll deal with it. I don't care what he says or does to me, as long as I get home to my babies and can take care of them. Jody won't stay alive if she doesn't get her fluids, and the little ones need to be syringe-fed, and there is so much cleaning to be done. I will just go home tomorrow and take care of them, and we'll be okay.

Yes, someone will come and get me tomorrow. I can make it through tonight. It's no big deal to sleep on a mattress on the floor with a room full of people I don't know. Just as long as I can get home to take care of my furkids, I'll be okay. We'll all be okay.

~ ~ ~

At 6:00 a.m., a corrections officer came through the steel door and started calling people to give them their medications. One by one, girls stumbled from their cells or got up off their mattresses and went to the doorway to be given their pills. The CO would watch them swallow and then make a mark on a sheet of paper. She would then wheel a steel cart through the doorway that had cartons of milk and juice and cereal, and one by one the girls took food and either found seats at the steel tables or took their food back to their cells and ate on their bunks.

I waited and prayed and waited all day, waiting for someone to come through the steel door to tell me I was going home. I must have looked at that steel door a thousand times. Every time it opened, I would think, *Okay, this is it. This is when I get to go home.*

I was wrong. Days passed, and I stopped looking so often at the steel door for someone to save me.

~ ~ ~

Some girls were released; some were sent to other jails or rehab places. All I know is that a bed opened up, and there was a place for me that wasn't on the floor. I was assigned a top bunk in a cell with two other girls. They taught me how to get up to the top bunk: Stand on the toilet seat, climb onto the sink, and hoist yourself up to the mattress on the steel-framed bunk. To get down you'd do everything the same, only in reverse. Unless you were really talented, and then you could avoid the sink and toilet by sliding yourself over the edge of the bunk and catching one of your feet on the bottom bunk, lowering yourself down the rest of the way to the concrete floor.

When the corrections officers perceived that any inmates in one cell were getting too chummy or something, they would decide to move inmates to different cells, to "mix it up," I guess. I soon was moved to another cell—the one that Cheryl was in—and assigned to the top bunk.

Cheryl was sleeping on a mattress on the floor next to the bunks, and I soon learned that she chose to be on the floor when the cell block was overcrowded because she said it was "easier" for her to get up and down from the floor, and she couldn't even try the top bunk. I also soon learned that Cheryl was in poor health—she was diabetic. She had to have her blood sugar tested twice a day, and she was taking medications. Cheryl was very short, petite, had chin-length gray hair, a couple of broken front teeth and wore glasses. She read a lot and introduced me to James Patterson novels when we were able to borrow books from the library, which was a small closet off the gym.

Cheryl also loved to play cards to try to pass the time, and she loved to talk about where she had been, what she had seen, and what she had done in her past life. I learned that she came from a hardworking family that insisted she work hard for what she had. She had traveled extensively around the world and had toured Europe when she was younger. I learned that she was a nurse, that she had been madly in love with her former boyfriend for many years, and that they had moved from their hometown of Scranton, Pennsylvania, to the Florida Panhandle at one point in their relationship. She told me they had a beautiful home, they had joint savings and retirement accounts, and she worked for some time as a dialysis nurse.

Cheryl would tell me detailed stories of her trips and the years she spent with her boyfriend, whom she always assumed would one day be her husband. She also told me how they eventually went their separate ways because they had come to an impasse, realizing that they both wanted different things for their futures. It was so obvious that it was very painful for her to talk about, but I believe she never stopped loving him. It helped so much to hear her stories, especially about her travels; and it was often the only diversion during the course of our very long days. She was very intelligent, did not seem crazy to me in any way, and had lived a wonderfully full and productive life.

She also talked about her animals, and every time she did, she would cry. She said she missed them desperately, and she knew how much I agonized over being away from mine. She told me she had trained Great Danes for many years and, to Cheryl, there was no other animal quite like them. She also had cats over the years, but her fondness for her dogs was so much greater. She told me she would show Great Danes at AKC competitions—dogs that belonged to other owners—and you could see the pride on her face when she talked about those times. She told me the names of all her dogs, and I eventually named a couple of my rescue cats after two of Cheryl's Great Danes—Snickers and Smoochie.

To this day, I struggle terribly with the accusations and charges that Cheryl left her Great Danes to starve to death by locking them in kennels without food and leaving them for days or weeks at a time. Cheryl told me that she and her mother were being evicted from their home because the mortgage was being foreclosed, and that she was trying to move her mother and herself from Bradford back to their hometown of Scranton. She told me she was arrested when she threatened a police officer or some other law enforcement person for threatening her mother on their property, and that her dogs died while she was in custody. I didn't know what to believe at the time, but I know for certain that something like that *could* happen. *I know.*

~ ~ ~

A few days after being moved into Cheryl's cell, I was trying to get down from my top bunk one afternoon and tried using the avoid-the-sink-and-toilet maneuver. I slid myself over the side of the bunk, trying to catch my foot on the lower bunk. I had the required white socks on my feet, and my foot didn't quite catch on the steel frame of the bunk but instead slipped right over it. I tried to grab my blanket to catch myself, but it didn't do any good. I fell straight backward and down, perfectly hitting the center of my spine on the edge of the steel desk mounted to the wall opposite my bunk. I then fell on Cheryl on her mattress on the floor and then onto the concrete floor.

I remember screaming, and I remember being terrified that I had broken my back. I was afraid to move, and I think Cheryl had to push me off of her to get up herself. I had knocked her glasses off, and knocked the wind out of her. Some of the other girls came in to see what was going on, and someone called for the CO. They eventually brought the jail nurse to check on me, and she looked at my back once, told them to get me some Tylenol and an ice pack, and then left.

I never saw her again. Within a few hours, there was a huge swollen area in the center of my back, and it eventually turned into a huge bruise. I was in a lot of pain for many days afterward but was told by the other inmates that there was no point in trying to get any kind of treatment or tests for any injury, because I wouldn't get it. I knew if I was home and had injured my back, I would have gone for X-rays. I was fifty-five and knew I wouldn't heal as fast as the younger girls. I was often told by the other inmates that they considered you to be a troublemaker if you disrupted the routine or asked for anything they considered out of the ordinary, and you could get written up for complaining.

~ ~ ~

Jody got really sick—Jody, the corrections officer. But Jody the CO didn't want to stay home, or couldn't stay home, or whatever. Jody came to work in the cell block really sick, with a really bad upper respiratory infection. I would find out much later that the McKean County Jail's female cell block had been designed and built to "house" five inmates initially. Then it had been "expanded" to house seven inmates, not by physically expanding it, but by turning a room meant for one thing into a cell to house two more inmates. The cell block had never been physically expanded, just *mentally* expanded, I guess. Like in the minds of the people running the jail, they thought it was an OK idea to house more than five or seven inmates at one time. During my incarceration, the population of the women's cell block rose to twenty-one, though it was usually fifteen to eighteen.

The women's cell block had no windows. Well, there were windows, but with glass blocks from top to bottom. There was no view of the outside world, and there was absolutely no way to get any fresh air. It was like living in a huge concrete closet with steel furniture and steel bars and a huge mirror through which "they" could watch you, but you couldn't watch a thing. It was like living in a huge concrete closet with at least fifteen other women, most of whom don't like you.

The day after Jody came to work really sick, more than half of the female inmates started getting sick. Some got mildly sick, some got really sick. Cheryl and I got really sick. We both came down with horrific sore throats and coughs we couldn't stop. Fever, headaches, muscle aches, sweating, and chills. I asked for "something" from the nurse, and they said "nothing" was ordered, so I couldn't get "something." I could have some Tylenol, but they couldn't give me anything else unless it was ordered by the prison doctor. I had never seen a prison doctor, nor did I know there was such a person. I asked if I could see the prison doctor, and never saw one.

Well, that's not quite true. Nearly three weeks after I got really sick, and was still really sick, I was called to the prison doctor's office one evening after supper, and I remember thinking, *Oh, thank God! At least now I'm going to get something!* The prison doctor sat at a small desk with a checklist, making check marks with a pen on his checklist. I was given a TB test and was told I could go back to my cell.

I looked at the prison doctor and the prison nurse and said, "I thought I was going to get something."

"For what?" they asked.

I told them I'd been sick for weeks, and the nice prison doctor said he could order me some kind of decongestant. That was it. Nothing else. Sorry.

~ ~ ~

I have attached a copy of a pencil drawing I made while I was in Cheryl's cell for the remaining five weeks of my incarceration. Cheryl was on the floor next to my bunk.

Lockdown

THERE ARE SO many things that are hard to describe to anyone who hasn't had the experience themselves. One of the terrifying things I learned in jail was what it was like to be in jail, and then be even more imprisoned in jail. In jail I learned when to try to be hungry, when to hope to watch the television on the wall, when to try to go to the bathroom on the toilet in the cell where everyone is trying to read or sleep or eat, with no privacy and no modesty. I found that it is a truly terrifying feeling, no matter how many times you experience it, to have a CO come to your cell at "bedtime" and slide those heavy steel doors shut to remind you that you are in a cage. To hear the electronic buzzer locking everyone in, and then to start praying that the next day someone who loves you will come and rescue you, and to pray that you won't start having panic attacks again because you can't run away from them, or to pray that your restless leg syndrome won't start attacking you because you can't get up and walk it out or walk it off. There was no place to walk in a five-by-eight-foot cell with Cheryl on the mattress on the floor and a toilet and a sink taking up almost all the rest. And if your throat is sore, you have to drink the crappy warm water out of the nasty sink because you can't get to the bathtub all night to get something colder.

I didn't know that I would get punished if another inmate acted up or acted out. But when one girl started swearing and pacing and threatening and screaming, the first thing that the CO did was order everyone back to their own cells from the day room and lock us down. She explained that the rule was that if one was bad, all would be punished. So the girl who was misbehaving got locked down for forty-eight excruciatingly long damnable hours, and so did everyone else, and so did I.

Lockdown happened more than once, but the other times, it was only for twenty-four excruciatingly long damnable hours. It is so hard to explain, unless you've "been there, done that" how panic can just overtake you in a split second when you know you can't move or can't scream or can't make a decision or can't talk to someone who cares about you. It is one of the most frightening things I have ever experienced, and I can't imagine how someone who has no faith and nothing otherworldly to believe in could even survive it without literally going mad.

I cried every day I was in that horrible place, and it would always be so much worse at the end of the day, when your cell door was locked and all you had was a terrible flat pillow, a scratchy wool blanket, a stained white sheet, and your thoughts exploding in your head. I would cry as quietly as I could, because the other inmates don't ever want to hear anyone crying, and every night I would stroke the palm of my hand along the green concrete-block wall, eyes closed, pretending I was stroking my oldest cat, Buster. I would imagine I was telling him, "Mama loves you, and I'm never going to leave you again, and it's going to be all right. We're going to get through this." I had no idea what my Buster, and his brothers and sisters, were going through right then. Thank God I didn't know then.

~ ~ ~

I began writing letters—to everyone and anyone I could think of. I wrote to the president judge of the county, John Cleland. I had not only known him for many years through my husband's work with and for the county, but I had known him since I was a child. Our families were members of the same country club—the one that had horseback riding instead of golf—and I had known John Cleland by his nickname, "Jocko." He was an equestrian, as were my twin brothers. He came from money, and we didn't.

John Cleland not only went on to become our President Judge, but later in his career, as an appellate court judge, oversaw one of our state's most infamous child-molestation cases against former Penn State coach Jerry Sandusky. Hopefully you will come to see the irony of John Cleland working so hard to protect my porn-addicted husband from the press and the public and then going on to oversee a case where one of the most outrageous components was that the Penn State "powers-that-be" worked so hard to cover up for a child molester.

I also wrote to the three county commissioners often. John Egbert was the chairman of the Board of Commissioners, a local businessman with family money and many connections.

I wrote to the district attorney, John Pavlock, who was subsequently appointed an interim judge when the county was lacking a second judge, and was thereafter elected to a ten-year term as president judge by the voters.

And I wrote and wrote and wrote to the *Bradford Era*, the local newspaper, which was owned and run by John Satterwhite, a man of substantial family wealth and, although it doesn't need to be said, substantial connections in the community.

At the time of all my letter-writing, I had no idea what was going on behind the scenes, among all these powerful men with all their powerful connections. I would find out the depth of the corruption and collusion much later.

~ ~ ~

Learning to Be an Inmate

I LEARNED SO much about being in that jail very quickly.

I learned that more than half of the female inmates were clients of my husband's, or of my husband's Office of the Public Defender.

I learned that most of the inmates thought I was an informant, or a plant. I often heard things like "No lawyer would have his wife sent to jail" and "No lawyer would leave his wife in jail." I was regularly threatened and mocked by the other inmates because they never believed I was a real inmate.

I learned that at any given time, the majority of the female inmates were either drug users, drug dealers, or both. They would freely talk about using drugs, selling drugs, or buying drugs, even though there was a huge one-way mirror between the cell block and the CO's office, and the COs could hear everything that was being said.

I learned that most of the younger girls who were *alleged* drug users or dealers referred to themselves as "gay," and several considered themselves married to another female, even though gay marriage in Pennsylvania wasn't yet legal. But then, neither was dealing or using illicit drugs. One young girl who had apparently recently converted to homosexuality had four children, and I believe they were all conceived with males.

I learned very quickly that you didn't complain to the warden or the assistant warden or the COs or to anyone. I was often told you would get "written up" if you complained.

~ ~ ~

After I'd been in jail about four or five days, Officer Mike Ward came to see me. He said he wanted to "interview" me. The interview was very strange. He started out by telling me that my husband wanted more charges filed against me. He said Ron had a *team* of lawyers working with him, and that they were having meetings and trying to figure out how they could keep me in jail as long as possible. I asked him who the team of lawyers was, and he told me that he knew for sure that Greg (Henry) and Chris (Hauser) were spending time with Ron, having discussions about what could be done to me. He told me that it seemed really important to them that more charges were filed while I was still in jail, and very specifically said "I'm supposed to file more charges so you won't be able to get out of jail."

~ ~ ~

November 14, 2007

Twelve days had passed since I had been crammed into an overcrowded cell block, and it had been 24-hour-a-day agony. I was so terrified for my animals. I was becoming more and more afraid for myself and my own safety. I would frantically try to make phone calls from the cellblock and rarely got through to anyone. I had tried to call my youngest daughter at her home and never got an answer. I had tried to call her at work – at our office – and I would only get recordings saying my calls were blocked to that number. I tried to call my oldest daughter and she couldn't accept my calls until she set up some special kind of prepaid account that would allow them to go through and, once she set it up, I would often dial her number and the call just wouldn't go through at all.

After a couple of weeks, my best friend of thirty years did set up an account for me to call her but would later let me know she thought it was really going out of her way to do it. She didn't like the stress of having to deal with my situation, and would have rather I left her alone until I got home. Most of the time, when I tried to call her, my call was never answered.

~ ~ ~

November 14 was going to be a *huge* day for me. It was going to be the beginning of the end of my torment in jail, and I was going to be able to go home to care for my animals again. I was beside myself with hope, fear, panic, anything you could imagine feeling when you have no idea what is going to happen. I was terrified that when I got home I would find my animals dead. I was terrified that I would literally have no home, since I knew my husband had already locked me out of the office and could well have locked me out of our home as well.

I did not sleep the night before. I tossed and turned and looked at my watch every ten or fifteen minutes. When I was finally so exhausted that I started to fall asleep, I realized it was almost 6:00 a.m. In jail, you are *allowed* to get up at 6:00 a.m., and you are also *required* to get up at 6:00 a.m. The corrections officers distribute medications at 6:00 a.m. and shortly after that, they wheel in the food cart for breakfast.

I ate little. I desperately wanted to get in the shower before anyone else. I knew that my preliminary hearing was scheduled for 9:00 a.m., and there was no way in this hell I was not going to be ready to go. I showered and dressed in my prison oranges and combed my hair nonstop for about an hour, trying to get it to dry. There are no hair dryers in jail.

I sat on my bunk and waited. I sat on a steel stool at the steel table and waited. It was well past eight o'clock and still no one had called or come for me. I started feeling really sick, and even more scared, but I just kept thinking and hoping that they must just be running behind.

When it was closing in on 9:00 a.m., I asked to speak to the CO on duty. Connie came to the door, and I asked her when they were going to come get me. She asked me where I was supposed to be going. Oh, no! *How could she not know?*

I told her I had a hearing scheduled for that morning, and I thought someone would be coming to get me. She told me she would check and see what was going on. She came back within a few minutes and told me that she didn't see a request or order for me to be taken to a hearing. I started shaking and crying, and she told me she would call Cercone's office and ask them what was going on, if there was a mix-up.

Connie came back to the cell block and told me that Cercone's secretary had told her that I wasn't on the docket for that morning. I was really frantic now and went to get my papers that said specifically that I had a preliminary hearing scheduled for *that* morning. Connie said she would call them back, and she did. She came back again after another few minutes and told me she had spoken to Cercone herself, and that he told her I wasn't going to get a hearing, that he was continuing it. I had no lawyer, and no one had notified me that anything was being continued, and I was now sobbing. I told Connie I didn't care about having the preliminary hearing; I would be just as happy with a hearing to have my bail reinstated.

Connie called Cercone's office back one more time and came back to tell me she had again spoken to Dom Cercone, who said he had *no* intention of giving me a hearing or reinstating my bail.

I had no attorney. I had no one to complain to. I had no one to ask what was going on. I had no one! I just remember leaning against the concrete block wall, sobbing and then sliding down the wall onto the floor. I was beyond hysterical. I was absolutely terror-stricken.

Cheryl came running out of our cell and started yelling at me. She told me I would get written up if I didn't settle down, and then walked me back into the cell. I knew she honestly cared about me, and she had been there much longer than I was, so she knew all too well how the place ran and what the unspoken rules were.

Cheryl kept telling me she didn't think I understood what I was most likely going to go home to, what I was going to find at home. She kept telling me that what was happening to me was much worse than I realized. Cheryl was right.

I never got an explanation about what had happened the day my preliminary hearing was supposed to be held. But I would find out, several weeks later, that although I had no attorney, Dominic Cercone was going to make sure I stayed in that cell; and he would literally go on to falsify official court documents to try to make it look like it was all legitimate. He could not let anyone know that Chris Hauser and Greg Henry and my own husband had asked him to strip me of all my rights and figuratively rape me, over and over again. They deprived me of every constitutionally protected right I was to be afforded. He could not let anyone know that he had much more power and control over my very life than anyone could have ever imagined. And if he had so much power and control over *my* life, how much power and control did he have over other people's lives?

~ ~ ~

I have attached copies of three court documents so you can clearly see how Dominic Cercone falsified official records to keep me imprisoned:

The first is a court order signed by Judge John Yoder, our second county court judge, appointing Attorney James Martin to represent me with respect to the simple assault case. It is clearly dated November 16, 12007. Until November 16, 2007, I had no lawyer.

The second is a notice of continuance for the hearing that was supposed to be held on November 14, 2007. At the bottom, you can see that Dom Cercone back-dated this form by not signing it until November 26, 2007, and misrepresenting that I had a lawyer on November 14 that requested a continuance of the matter. That is a lie. I had no lawyer on November 14.

The third is another notice of continuance, also signed by Dom Cercone on November 26, 2007, again misrepresenting that my attorney requested a continuance of the hearing scheduled for November 28, 2007. Dom Cercone signed both of these continuances on November 26, 2007, and I did not receive either one until I was released from jail on December 12, 2007.

COMMONWEALTH OF PENNSYLVANIA   IN THE COURT OF COMMON PLEAS
                                      OF McKEAN COUNTY, PENNSYLVANIA
              VS.

CATHERINE F. LANGELLA   CTN: K 697838-1 747 CR2007

                            O R D E R

        AND NOW, this 16th day of November ____, 2007, upon

consideration of the foregoing Petition to Appoint Counsel,

James L. Martin, Esquire, ____ is hereby appointed as

counsel to represent the above-named Defendant in any and all

further Court proceedings.

                        BY THE COURT:

                        _____
                        JUDGE

                              c: D A
                                 J Martin
                                 P D
                                 D. Cousins, DJ

COMMONWEALTH OF PENNSYLVANIA
COUNTY OF: **MCKEAN**

NOTICE OF CONTINUANCE

Mag. Dist. No.   **48-1-01**

MDJ Name: Hon.

DOMINIC A. CERCONE, JR
Address: **22 DAVIS ST**
UNION SQ
BRADFORD, PA
Telephone: **(814) 368-4075   16701**

COMMONWEALTH OF

PENNSYLVANIA

VS.

DEFENDANT: NAME and ADDRESS
LANGELLA, CATHERINE F.
236 E. MAIN STREET
BRADFORD, PA 16701

DOMINIC A. CERCONE, JR
22 DAVIS ST
UNION SQ
BRADFORD, PA 16701

L

Docket No.: **CR-0000313-07**
Date Filed: **10/22/07**

X 697838-1

Please note that the hearing in the above captioned case, which was scheduled to occur on: **11/14/07**

has been continued to:

Date:	11/28/07	Place:	DISTRICT COURT 48-1-01
			22 DAVIS ST
Time:	11:00 AM		
			UNION SQ
			BRADFORD, PA 16701

If you have any questions, please contact this office immediately.   *He was not my attorney on that date*

Continuance requested by: **MARTIN, JAMES L**

If you are disabled and require assistance, please contact the Magisterial District office at the address above.

11/26/07 Date   *Dominic A. Cercone Jr.*   Magisterial District Judge

My commission expires first Monday of January,

DOMINIC CERCONE SAYS MR. MARTIN
REQUESTED CONTINUANCE

COMPLAINT NUMBER:
AOPC 610-06

DATE PRINTED: 11/26/07 10:02:34 AM
DATE COMPLAINT SIGNED: 10/22/07

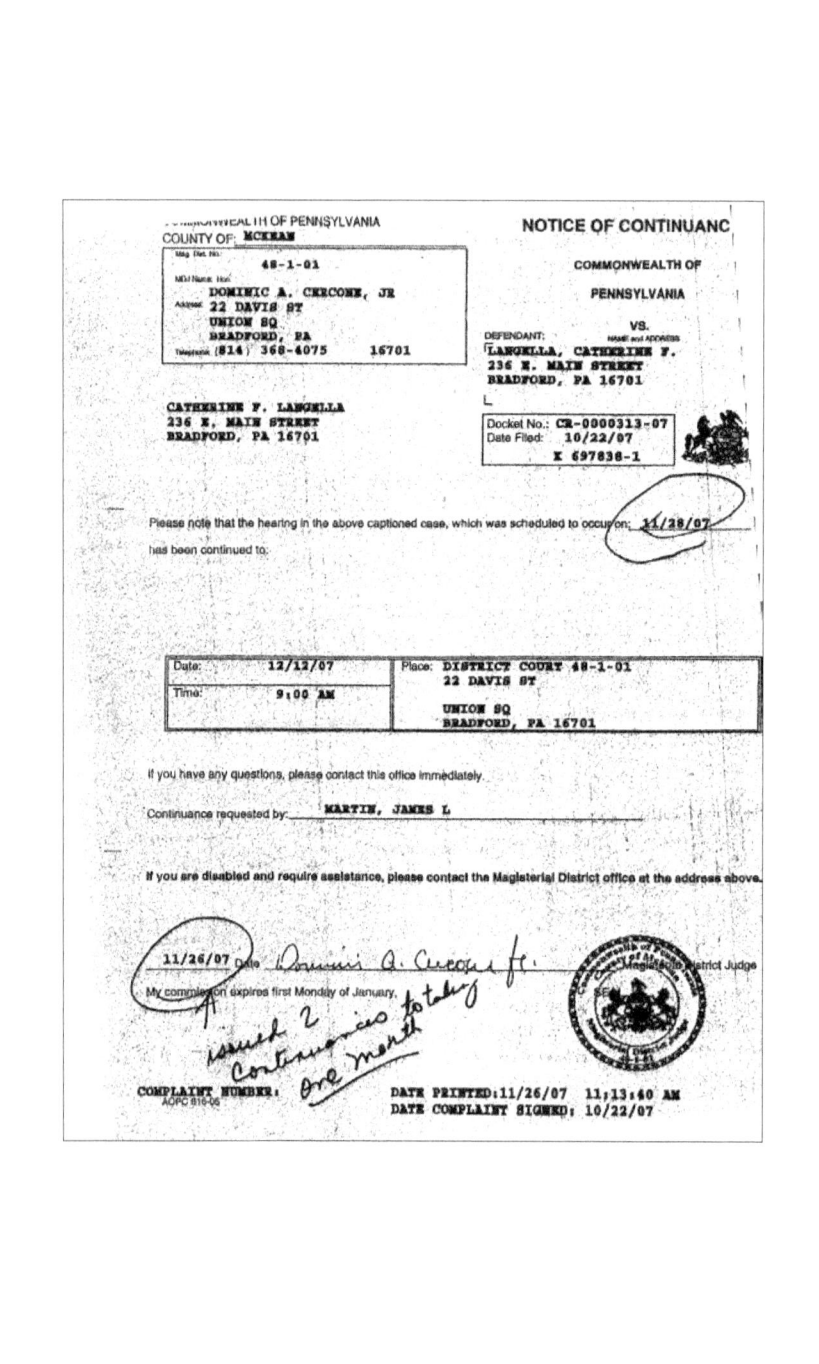

COMMONWEALTH OF PENNSYLVANIA
COUNTY OF: **MCKEAN**

NOTICE OF CONTINUANC

Mag. Dist. No.:
48-1-01

MDJ Name: Hon.
DOMINIC A. CECONE, JR
Address: 22 DAVIS ST
UNION SQ
BRADFORD, PA
Telephone: (814) 368-4075   16701

COMMONWEALTH OF
PENNSYLVANIA

VS.

DEFENDANT: NAME and ADDRESS
LANGELLA, CATHERINE F.
236 N. MAIN STREET
BRADFORD, PA 16701

CATHERINE F. LANGELLA
236 N. MAIN STREET
BRADFORD, PA 16701

Docket No.: CR-0000313-07
Date Filed: 10/22/07
         X 697838-1

Please note that the hearing in the above captioned case, which was scheduled to occur on: **11/28/07**

has been continued to:

Date:	12/12/07	Place: **DISTRICT COURT 48-1-01**
Time:	9:00 AM	**22 DAVIS ST**
		UNION SQ
		BRADFORD, PA 16701

If you have any questions, please contact this office immediately.

Continuance requested by: _____**MARTIN, JAMES L**_____

If you are disabled and require assistance, please contact the Magisterial District office at the address above.

11/26/07 Date _____ Magisterial District Judge

My commission expires first Monday of January,

issued 2 Continuances to today. One month

COMPLAINT NUMBER:
AOPC 816-06

DATE PRINTED: 11/26/07   11:13:40 AM
DATE COMPLAINT SIGNED: 10/22/07

Mike Olearchick

I "met" Michael Olearchick at the McKean County Jail three days after I was incarcerated. I knew him well, but I had no idea he was working at the jail. I had been asked if I would like to see a counselor since I was having a very "difficult" time, and I was thrilled that I'd be able to talk to someone that might be able to help me get out. I just kept thinking that if someone knew what had really happened, they would go to one of the judges or get me a lawyer or *something*. I was called out of the cell block to see this "counselor," and when I walked into the little conference room with the table and a couple of chairs, I was *so* happy to see Mike there! I threw my arms around him, sobbing, and started begging him to help me.

You see, Michael Olearchick was not only the "jail counselor," but the year before, Mike had been counseling my husband and me for many months in his capacity as a therapist/counselor at the Guidance Center. Mike Olearchick knew all about the money that I'd taken from my husband's account, and Mike Olearchick also knew that my husband had been abusive, threatening, and that he not only had a serious problem with anger management, but was a serious pornography addict. To his credit, when we were in counseling sessions, my husband had been brutally honest with Mike while I sat there with him. After months of counseling sessions with Mike, he told us that he didn't think it was going to do any good to keep seeing the two of us together but rather wanted to keep seeing my husband one-on-one to attempt to help him with his addictions and anger management issues. He suggested that if my husband was able to make some progress in counseling, we might have a better chance of working things out.

Now Mike Olearchick was a counselor at the jail, and I thought I had just run into a friend in the worst place I'd ever been in my life. I honestly believed that Mike would be calling my husband or calling *someone* before the end of that day, and I'd be going home—with his help.

Instead, Mike turned out to be another company man. He had a job he was going to protect, and he wasn't going to do a damn thing to help me. I am attaching a copy of the notes Mike put in my file at the jail after seeing me twice in two weeks. When I first read it, I felt physically ill, and it's still not easy to read.

Mike wrote about me like I was on vacation. He said I was "talking and hanging out" with other inmates! He said I "reported no other problems"! Like I wasn't complaining too much about the room service other than the fact that I didn't like the food there.

Mike also wrote that I had "continued anger towards" my husband.

What Mike had done was exactly what others would eventually do. I learned that when you are in the McKean County Jail, the people that work there *never* talk about or report what really goes on there. If you keep reading, you will see that this was a practice that was most likely taught to the employees. They were to say we were all doing great and there's "nothing to see here."

I was honestly heartbroken that he turned on me for his job. He never did one damn thing to try to help me, or to put in my file anything that would give a clue as to what was really going on with me. He never even mentioned my rescues, and anyone who spent any time with me at all in that jail knew that I was terrified for them every minute I was there. He didn't write about my fall or that I was sick. He didn't write that I was regularly being threatened by the other inmates because they thought I was an informant. He didn't write that he knew my husband well and that he knew I had been terrorized by him for almost two years.

Mike knew all those things, and he never said a word.

Mike Olearchick was a coward.

~ ~ ~

Below is a copy of Mike Olearchick's notes. Since I received these notes through a Request for Production of Documents during the course of my lawsuit against the county, it is my belief that Mike attempted to reconstruct his notes from two years before, and therefore wrongly dated them.

Inmate C. Langella #97

11/5/2009- This counselor met with inmate Langella at her request. Inmate was crying and upset about being in jail and stated that she "doesn't belong here'. This counselor offered support and discussed visitation, rules and available programs at the jail. This counselor told inmate to put in a request if she needed to talk in the future.

[signature]

Michael Olearchick, M.S.ED.
Jail Counselor

11/19/2009- This counselor met with inmate Langella at her request. Inmate stated that she was adjusting better yet did not like the food here. Inmate stated that some of the other female inmates were saying things to her about her husband being a public defender yet there were other inmates that she is talking and hanging out with. Inmate's overall adjustment appears to be good. She reports no other problems at this point other than wanting to get out of jail and some continued anger towards her husband.

[signature]

Michael Olearchick, M.S.ED.
Jail Counselor

Marcie Schellhammer

I had been writing to the *Bradford Era* since the first few days I was in jail. After my husband and I had the "altercation" in our office, I had talked to Marty Wilder, the city editor, who expressed shock and sympathy toward me. Her words to me turned out to be less than sincere.

I was writing desperate letters to the newspaper, telling them what was happening to me and begging them to help me. Marcie Schellhammer had been a reporter at the *Era* for years and was "allowed" to visit me while I was incarcerated, but didn't come until I'd been there over a month. She came with a notepad and a pen and talked to me through the glass in the visiting area.

I had all of my paperwork and notes organized and was so hopeful—again—that maybe this time I was going to get some help. I was sobbing as I described to her what was going on and showed her the court paperwork I had from Cercone's office. I was showing her *proof* that Dom Cercone had falsified an official court document. I was showing her *proof* that I had been repeatedly denied either a bail hearing or a preliminary hearing. Marcie had been covering the court docket long enough to know that I was entitled to a hearing long before she was seeing me.

Marcie did her best to act shocked and surprised. "Oh, my God!" she said several times. Marcie also knew very well that I had dozens of rescues I had been taking care of for years. Like so many others, Marcie not only knew because my fights with my neighbors and the city had been very public at City Hall, but Marcie also knew because the *Era* had covered every detail, and quite often made me sound like some kind of crazy person for wanting to care for homeless animals.

Before Marcie left, she told me how sorry she was for me, and that she was going to see what she could do to help me. She said she would do her best to get back to see me as soon as she could.

Unfortunately, I had forgotten that Marcie had been good friends with Dom Cercone's wife, Pat, at the *Bradford Era*. If I had remembered she was friends with Pat, I'd have known that she would never help me.

I never saw Marcie again in jail, and you will see in later chapters why Marcie never came back, why she *couldn't* come back.

Final PFA Hearing

December 5, 2007

SINCE I HAD been living with threats of every kind from my husband for a long time, I believed it would be smart for me to ask the court for a protection from abuse order that would keep *him* away from *me*. After he had me charged with assault in October I met with women that worked at the local YWCA in their crisis counseling offices. One of them had helped me fill out the required paperwork and took me to the courthouse to meet with a judge to ask for a temporary order of protection, which I was able to get. It would only be good for a certain number of days, and if I didn't appear at a final hearing I would not be granted a final protection order. Judge Millin of Warren County was appointed to oversee my petition.

~ ~ ~

I was notified by jail staff that the final PFA hearing on my petition was still going to be heard today. I really didn't expect it. Everything I had asked to be scheduled had been denied. As soon as it sank in that it was going to be held, I was again overwhelmed with so many emotions. I was scared. So scared. I wanted to be hopeful that this was at least a chance that I would get a final, permanent order of protection. I tried to recall the judge that had approved my temporary protection order. Was he nice to me? Did he seem to be fair? I couldn't remember. It now seemed like a lifetime ago that Mickey had taken me to see him, asking that he hear my petition for protection from abuse, asking him to give me at least a temporary order of protection from my husband.

I prayed. I showered and put on clean prison oranges, white socks, and bright orange rubber sandals. I was sick to my stomach; I was shaking. I prayed more. Please, God. Please help me this time. I was still not well from the upper respiratory infection, which had lasted weeks. With no hair dryer in jail, I tried to get my hair as dry as I could with my only towel, knowing I had to go outside in the freezing cold. Well, I assumed it had to be cold out. It was the fifth of December, and although I hadn't been outside since the second of November, I knew that it was usually cold on the fifth of December.

Connie the CO came to get me from the cell block. Connie was always so nice to me, and I knew she didn't have to be, so it meant a lot. She took me to the booking room, and she got me "ready" to be transported. She told me to kneel on the wooden chair next to the desk. I looked at her as though I didn't understand. "Why?" She said it was the rules. Policy. Standard procedure. She was sorry. She had to put shackles around my ankles. Oh my God. "Why?"

"Everyone has to be shackled and handcuffed to be transported."

Oh my God! I had hit my husband after years of torture and abuse, and I was now being shackled and handcuffed. His words again echoed in my throbbing head. "You think they will believe *you* over *me*? You have *got* to be kidding!" I was shaking so badly, I was praying so hard. *Please, God, please help me.*

Connie told me she was sorry and wished me good luck. I knew she meant it. I knew that, even just a little bit, she cared about what happened to me. Connie said something into her walkie-talkie, and a buzzer sounded. A door lock clicked. She opened the door into the garage, and I was told to get into the back seat of the police car.

It *was* freezing. It had recently snowed, so there was a lot of snow on the ground. It was so strange to see so much light and so much snow. I had been in a cell block for five weeks, where there were no windows, and where we had no fresh air. It was almost culture shock. I don't know how else to describe it.

Now I was really scared. Much more scared than hopeful, or nervous. I had absolutely *no* idea what to expect. I did not have a lawyer. I did not know how a PFA hearing went. What should happen, what to expect. I had no clue. I knew that Mickey said she would meet me there, and I hoped she would know what to do, what I was supposed to do. Today she was my lifeline to the real world.

The police car was parked at the curb, and I had to walk down a long sidewalk to get into the courthouse. I was wearing white socks and orange rubber sandals. It was still snowing. The snow was at least four inches deep, even on some of the sidewalks. By the time I walked the length of the sidewalk, my feet were totally soaked and freezing. I was wearing only prison oranges, which consisted of a pair of cotton duck pants and a pullover shirt. I had no sweater or jacket, nothing to warm me. Of course, there were the shackles around my ankles.

I was taken up a set of back stairs that must have only been used for prisoners, since the holding cell next to the courtroom was at the top of those stairs. It took me a minute to actually figure out where I was. I had been in that courthouse literally hundreds of times, mostly working with my husband. I had never noticed that holding cell next to the courtroom.

I was told to sit down in the holding cell, that they would get me when it was my turn. The cell was about four feet by eight feet, with one long wooden bench and nothing else that I can remember. I was still shackled and handcuffed; my feet were soaking wet and frozen, and I was shaking so badly. Trembling, crying. *Please, God. Please help me now! Please help me get through this!*

At some point, I was told that they were running behind in court and I would have to wait. I was really starting to feel so much more than scared or panicked or freezing. I was starting to feel really sick—sick to my stomach, my head pounding, shaking and dizzy. Mickey had stopped in for a few minutes, trying to calm me down, telling me she wasn't sure what to expect. She told me my husband was in the courtroom, and that he was with his lawyer. She seemed really concerned. No, concerned was not how she seemed. She seemed much more than concerned. She looked worried, and maybe even resigned. I think she knew that this wasn't going to be good for me, that there was going to be no good outcome for me.

The heavy door finally opened, maybe after about an hour. There were two sheriff's deputies standing there—court security—and they told me it was time for my hearing. Still shackled and handcuffed, soaking wet and frozen, my long hair unstyled and disheveled, graying from missing my regular hairdresser appointments. I was taken through the double doors into the courtroom, and I immediately looked to my left. At the prosecution table was my husband and his lawyer and "best friend," Greg. All on the same side of the room, behind and around him, were his colleagues, associates, and longtime friends. Court employees, jail staff, onlookers.

On the right side of the courtroom, reserved for me, was *no one*. I moaned, "Oh, my God! Why are you all doing this to me?" and started to collapse onto the floor. Two deputies grabbed both of my arms and took me back out into the hallway. "You will either get yourself together, or you will get no hearing!"

Oh my God. Where was my God? I was right. I was in hell. I was sobbing and could barely stand. My husband and his "lawyer" were both dressed in suits and ties. All the onlookers were in appropriate clothing, hair combed and no one with soaking, frozen feet in rubber sandals. Why was I? Because I had hit my husband, and he was a lawyer. Because he told me, "No one will ever believe you over me!" Because he was right.

I was asked several times if I wanted to be taken back to the jail and not have the hearing. I was taken back to the holding cell and told I would be given a chance to get myself together. Mickey came to talk to me, tried to calm me down, and said she would do what she could to help me. I did not want to give up my chance to go before the court and ask for an order of protection. I was taken back to the courtroom, in handcuffs and shackles.

I was told to sit at the defense table, on the right side of the courtroom, opposite all the people who surrounded my husband. I sat down, alone. Mickey was seated in the back of the courtroom, behind me. She never spoke a word throughout the entire "hearing."

Judge Millin addressed me, and I can't remember much of what he said at the outset. I was so overwhelmed by grief, fear, panic, terror. There just isn't one appropriate word to describe what was washing over my entire body. Waves of absolute terror. Little hope left. I looked at him and tried to focus my eyes to see if I might get a clue as to how he was going to treat me. I was trying to find some glimmer of hope that he might be nice to me.

"Mrs. Langella, you may proceed." I felt as though someone had punched me in the stomach. I had no idea what he meant, and I told him that. He went on to tell me that I was the one bringing the action, and that it was solely my responsibility to present my case. If I was going to get a protection from abuse order entered against my husband, I had to present my case. I had to *prove* my case.

I had no lawyer. None were willing to help me. Everyone had conflicts of interest unless I had a lot of money to hire someone. I had no witnesses. I did not know I was allowed to call witnesses. I didn't know anything at all about the process. Mickey had not told me what to expect. I know she didn't have a clue herself, because she had told me, on more than one occasion, that she had "never seen anything like this." Mickey had not told me that I should call witnesses. Mickey was sitting in the back of the courtroom, silently watching.

I do remember being called to the witness stand by my husband's lawyer, and I remember Greg asking me questions about how bad I was, how I had taken money from my husband, and how I had hit him. This was a man that I had known for twenty years and once considered a friend. This was a man that had made passes at me when I first started dating my husband, as he always made passes at just about every female he saw when he was drinking. And "when he was drinking" was pretty much all the time. He had spent time in federal prison for not filing tax returns or paying income taxes, and was a chronic alcoholic who had his own history of physical abuse against women. He often showed up in court, even in the mornings, with alcohol on his breath, wearing jeans and looking disheveled. This was a man who was famous for dating divorce clients while representing them, and even dated the wife of one of his divorce clients. He infamously dated the wife of a local doctor who had been charged with trying to kill his wife, and the doctor went on to fake his own death at Niagara Falls. When the doctor was arrested and it was found that he had worn rubber gloves to try to strangle his wife, he would try to explain that he took the rubber gloves to "demonstrate" to his wife how she should make Greg use a condom when they had sex. This was a man who was once our mayor, and had been criminally charged, during his tenure, for biting some guy in the stomach while he was drunk.

This was the man who had helped my husband try to destroy my very life, and was now talking to me like I was a piece of garbage.

After my husband was examined by his "friend," I was given permission to ask my husband my own questions.

"Have you ever threatened to kill me?"

"No."

"Have you ever threatened me with a knife?"

"No."

"Do you have any addictions?"

"No."

"Have you ever physically abused me?"

"No."

My husband was under oath, and he lied under oath. He answered every question with a lie.

After the phony question-and-answer session, Judge Millin addressed me. He explained to me that the burden of proof was on me. It was not up to my husband to prove his innocence; I had to prove his guilt. Judge Millin told me I had not done that.

My petition for a protection from abuse order was dismissed.

My entire soaking-wet, frozen, shackled, and handcuffed body was suddenly on fire. Waves of grief just washed over me—again and again. I could feel my head and face burning, the room spinning, my stomach so sick. The deputies immediately came over to my chair, stood me up, and escorted me from the courtroom. I was sobbing, and not one person there cared.

I don't remember much about the ride back to the jail, but I do remember being in the booking room, soaking wet, shaking and feeling half-dead, and Connie walking up to me. She asked me what happened. I wailed, "They dismissed my petition!" I was stumbling and sobbing. Connie gestured for me to follow her into the shower room, where there were no security cameras. She put her arms around me and kept repeating, "I am *so* sorry. I am *so* sorry." She whispered again what I had heard so many others say: "I've just never seen anything like this."

I was taken back to my cell. Back to my hell, where I was again just waiting to die. I was sure, again, that I would never leave that place alive.

I was again convinced that God had truly abandoned me. How could he ever love me and watch me go through all of this?

~ ~ ~

December 12, 2007
Another day of horrors

It was a Wednesday. The third time my preliminary hearing was supposed to be held on the simple assault and harassment charges filed against me by my husband on October 22. It had been nearly six weeks since I was jailed on November 2. I hardly slept all night and was the first in the cell block to get a shower. I was so scared, hopeful, afraid, excited. Praying, praying, praying. *Please, God, let my animals be okay. Please get me home to them. Please make them still be alive somehow. Please get me home to my own bed! Please get me home somehow!*

But I knew what had happened twice before. My hearings had been scheduled, and I had been denied those hearings. My public defender, eventually appointed from out of the county, had promised me the day before that I was going to get a hearing this time, but I had absolutely no reason to trust him either. By now, I knew they were all liars. By now I knew the whole system was corrupted far beyond what I had known and believed for so many years. I had learned so much by living every minute of my life with drug addicts and repeat offenders in that cell block. I had been living with so much fear that being afraid was just like breathing.

But this time the steel door to the cell block opened, and my name was called, along with several others. We were all taken to the booking room, where we were handcuffed and shackled. The rules. We were going to be taken into town for our court appearances.

We were all herded into the county jail van wearing orange pants and shirts, orange rubber sandals and white socks, and handcuffs and shackles. It was very cold and had obviously snowed lately because there were several inches of snow on the ground. The ride took about half an hour.

We were again herded together, this time into the district magistrate's office. I was terrified, but again praying for any kind of miracle I might be able to get. I was taken into the hallway and was told that my husband was there and wanted to talk to me. I was now much more terrified. I had no idea what he would try to do, and honestly did not know how to act. I just prayed again, but by this time could not be convinced that God was even listening.

My husband walked up to me and had a half-smile on his face. What did it mean? Was he going to be nice to me? Was he going to threaten me again? He asked "How are you?" and gave me a kiss on the cheek. I was wearing an orange prison outfit, my hair was unstyled, grown out and graying. I had lost nearly twenty pounds in six weeks, and was very weak and shaky. My husband was wearing a suit, white shirt and tie, and the really nice wool overcoat I'd bought him the year before for his birthday. He looked like a professional; I looked like death warmed-over.

I did my very best to smile and said, "I'm fine. I'm really good. I just want to go home." There was no way in hell I was going to give him the satisfaction of thinking that I was on the verge of losing my mind or breaking down or screaming.

He said, "You are going to go home today."

"Good!" I forced a smile. "I can't wait!" I could hardly breathe. My heart was pounding so hard I could hear it. I just knew I had to get through this somehow.

"I just want to make sure you're going to be able to handle it when you get there."

"I'm fine! I just want to get home and take care of the animals and sleep in my own bed."

He said again, "But I want to make sure you are going to be able to handle everything." I honestly had no idea what he was talking about, but did my best to continue the conversation. "I'll be fine."

"The house isn't in good shape."

"That's okay. I don't care."

"No. I don't think you understand. I had a really hard time keeping up with things, and it's really a mess. It's really bad. It was just too much work for me."

"That's okay. I'll take care of it."

I would have promised Satan he could have my soul that day to get home. I did not care that he kept telling me my house wasn't clean. Looking back on that day, and on so many things over so many years, it was not such a stretch to say that I was promising Satan anything he wanted just to keep myself and my animals from any more harm, just by making promises to my own husband.

Keep your friends close and your enemies closer. Okay, I can do that.

After a few minutes, my public defender came over to me and told me it was time for the hearing. I was taken to the defense table, and he sat down beside me. The courtroom was very small, and it was very full. There was another table for the prosecution, and I saw a familiar face: Todd Goodwin, from the Office of the Attorney General. He worked for Tom Corbett, the Pennsylvania Attorney General. I had seen him before. He had been specially assigned to take over the prosecution of my case because the district attorney, John Pavlock, felt he had a conflict of interest and wanted a special prosecutor appointed to handle the matter.

There was quite a bit of conversation between Cercone, my public defender, Todd Goodwin, and my husband, but it was out of earshot. Cercone then addressed me directly. He told me that there was "concern" that I should not be allowed to go home because they felt I was either a danger to myself or to others. He told me they had been discussing the possibility of a 302 involuntary commitment to a psychiatric facility to make sure I wasn't going to harm anyone. He "didn't feel good" about just letting me go home.

Oh my God! What is going to happen to me now? I thought I was going to stop breathing right there. Fear and panic just overwhelmed my entire body—again. My thoughts were racing. How could I get out of here? How can I get home? Can I run away? What about my animals? Where can I go? Please! Please, God! Please don't let them do anything else to me! *God, where are you?*

I desperately tried to compose myself. I told them all I was just fine. "Please, I just want to go home! I'll do anything they want me to do, just please let me go home! Please! I have sick animals that need me to take care of them!"

I heard my husband speak up. He was telling the judge he thought I would be okay. But they wanted me to understand that there were conditions that I would have to abide by, and there were circumstances that were going to make it hard for me. My husband told me he had taken my car, so I wouldn't have one. He said he had taken his truck off the road because it didn't have insurance, and I would have no way to get around. I heard myself saying it didn't matter. I had no idea what I was talking about, and wasn't even thinking I wouldn't be able to get things I needed for my animals, or to be able to get to an appointment or get my hair done or get a job. At that time, on that day, it didn't matter to me if I had a car. Or anything else. I just wanted to get myself the hell out of that place and find somewhere safe.

Cercone then started giving me a list of things I had to do if I wanted to be released. He would give me until 5:00 p.m. that day to get him a written statement from a psychiatrist that I was not a threat to myself or others. I told him my husband had just said he had taken my car and that I would have no way to get around. How was I going to do that?

Cercone smirked at me. "That's not my problem." He told me either I provided him with something from a psychiatrist by 5:00 p.m., or he would have to take another look at having me involuntarily committed. That day!

God! Please! Where are you? No answer. At least not that I heard. So I just kept trying to do whatever I thought I needed to do.

I said I would find a way. He then told me that there were going to be other conditions I'd have to strictly follow if I was going to be released. He told me that I could have absolutely no contact with my husband. He said not even through a third party. I was not allowed to contact him. For anything. If I even tried to contact him, I would go back to jail.

Oh, my God. I had personal things in the office that I needed. I would have to find a way to get things I needed to take care of the animals. I had no idea what I might need at home. I was sure my husband had some legal obligation to take care of us, at least to some extent. I had worked with him and helped him build his practice for nearly twenty years. I had worked so hard, so much harder than he ever did. I must be entitled to something, even if it was only for my rescues. But I knew that this was not the time to be thinking about those things. I just needed to get out of there and get home. I still had no idea how bad the house really was, or if my animals were okay. And I had been so worried about Jody and her subq fluids, and Buster and Jeter and the other sick ones…I just had to get home.

So I told Cercone, "Yes, sir. I understand."

~ ~ ~

We were all herded back into the van and were driven back to the jail, another half-hour trip. The handcuffs and shackles were removed. I was told to get my things together.

I could arrange for someone to pick me up, and I just had to wait for the paperwork to be processed to be released.

Cheryl came running out to meet me. She wanted to know what happened, was I going home? I told her I had to see a doctor, I had to get a ride, I had to do certain things. My head was spinning. I was terrified something else would go wrong, something else would happen to me. I had no idea what else they would try to do to me.

Then I really looked at Cheryl's face and saw she was crying. Oh my God! I was going to leave her there! She told me she didn't know what she would do without me, but that I shouldn't worry about her. She said her time was "almost up," and she was sure she'd get to go home to Scranton before Christmas. If a defendant hasn't been to trial within 180 days, the law requires that you are released on nominal bail—only $1. Speedy trial rule. Some speed. But Cheryl had been there just short of 180 days. She begged me to call her at the jail as soon as I got home. I was to call one of the corrections officers, and to let her know how I found things. She asked me to write to her, she said she'd write to me until she was able to leave. For a split second, I was hopeful for both of us. I thought maybe we were both going to have another chance to breathe fresh air, to not be locked in a five-foot-by-eight-foot cell, to wear *real* clothes, to have some kind of life left.

I felt so guilty leaving her there, like I was abandoning her.

The corrections officer gave me back the clothing I was wearing six weeks before when I was booked. I went into the shower room and got dressed. At first, I thought the clothes they gave me belonged to someone else. I pulled on my jeans, and they were hanging off me. I had been sick nearly the entire time I was there, had eaten very little, and there I was, with baggy jeans and a baggy shirt.

I was able to reach my oldest daughter on the phone, and she came to pick me up. As we were driving back to Bradford, I was acutely aware of how bright it was outside, that there was snow on the ground, that it was freezing cold, that I felt so frail and shaky and scared. My daughter attempted to make small talk with me, and I realized she was trying to prepare me for something. Just like my husband was earlier. She told me she and her husband had been stopping at my house once in a while to try to help clean things up and feed the cats, but that they weren't able to get everything done. I didn't care. I didn't care if it was bad. I just desperately wanted to go home and pick up my cats and hug and kiss them and tell them how much their mama loved them and missed them. I was going to promise them I'd never, ever leave them again.

~ ~ ~

Home! I ran up to the door of the family room and opened it. I stepped inside and didn't recognize where I was. At first I was almost disoriented, because it didn't look familiar. I tried to get my bearings. *What is different? What happened? Why does it hurt to breathe?*

Oh my God! My beautiful home! My new floors! My beautiful kitchen! *Oh my God!* Everything was destroyed!

I started screaming, running from room to room. My cats were running in every direction, I'm sure because my screaming scared the hell out of them. Oh my God! Who would do something like this? Who would allow this to happen? *I'm in hell again! Oh my God! I really did die and go to hell when I thought I did six freaking weeks ago!*

My home had been my dream house. I had designed and built a family room addition with a full bathroom and a beautiful new custom kitchen. I had renovated every single room, painting, and wallpapering, laying new flooring, oh-so-carefully picking out window treatments and finishes and just the right touches. It was all destroyed.

The stench in the entire house was indescribable. The air was putrid, burning, gag-inducing. Every single surface in my house was covered with animal feces and urine. The litter boxes that were still there had obviously not been scooped or changed in weeks. The litter inside them was solid black, soaked with urine hundreds of times over. The cats had obviously looked for clean places to go, so they went everywhere else. On countertops and appliances, in the whirlpool tubs and pedestal sinks, on my beds and new floors. On my clothing and towels and bedding. On plastic and wood and ceramic and glass. On everything, everywhere.

I found Buster, my oldest cat, standing in the middle of the kitchen floor. Buster was my furbaby that I would talk to quietly at night in my cell, and he was the one I would pretend to be stroking as I stroked the concrete block wall. He was nearly seventeen years old, with long, pure-white fur. He was a feral rescue I had trapped from under a building in town sixteen years before, and it had taken several years for him to become domesticated and trust me as his mama. Trust me to take care of him. Buster was now no longer white. He was red. He was heavily infested with fleas, and everywhere he had tried to bathe himself, the fur had turned red from the flea dirt. His long-haired white tail and back were covered with feces. I just picked him up and held him so tightly and kept saying, "Buster, Mama loves you! Mama is *so* sorry!"

I was no longer crying and screaming. I heard myself moaning and wailing in utter anguish and agony. I just kept running from room to room, holding Buster, wailing. Oh, my God! How could he do this to me? How could he do this to *them*? My husband often called our animals his babies. And he left them to suffer horrifically in abject squalor. If I used every word in a thesaurus that is similar to *squalor*, it would never be enough to describe what I found.

In the midst of my terror, I realized something really strange. My daughter did not seem to be surprised, or shocked, or much of anything. All of a sudden, I understood why. She had already seen this. She told me she had been coming to the house "once in a while," and she knew it was like this. Then I realized she was yelling at me to "stop" and "calm down," saying, "Mom, it's not that bad!" And, "Mom, stop overreacting!" She said, "Don't worry, we'll get it taken care of."

We will? Who is 'we'? How will 'we' take care of this?

She said she and her husband had tried to do some cleaning, but they just didn't have the time to get it all done. They lived half an hour away and had two kids and a house to take care of, and he had to work. I could not see that anything had been done there, ever. Not ever.

Oh Lord, this is my hell, isn't it? But why are you punishing these innocent animals? Why would you let this happen?

Then I remembered things I had to do. I only had until 5:00 p.m., or I was going back to jail, or worse. Cercone's office had arranged for me to see a psychiatrist at the Guidance Center at 5:00 p.m. to okay my release, to verify my sanity. Yeah, that should be easy, especially now.

I pulled myself together. Sort of. Not really. There were just things I had to do, and grieving would have to wait. I had immediately noticed that I didn't see Jody anywhere, and I was too terrified to ask if she was still alive. While I was in jail, my daughter had told me that Jody was getting her fluids, that she was okay, not to worry. My daughter later told me she lied to me because she didn't want me to be more upset than I already was. She lied to me about so many things.

Later that day, she told me that Jody had died, that she had found her behind the TV cabinet five days after I was jailed. Jody died believing her mama had abandoned her, waiting for her daily fluids, waiting for me to walk through the family room door at the end of the day so she could spin and twirl around my legs, cry to me for a pet, and sit on my lap for her sub-q drip. Jody had been abandoned by her mama, and she died alone, from kidney failure, convulsing and writhing and stiffening and shutting down, all alone. But I didn't have time to grieve for Jody either. I just had to shove the news out of my consciousness so I could keep myself from being jailed again, or worse.

My cell phone was dead and only had a few minutes on it anyways. I borrowed my daughter's phone and called the Guidance Center to confirm my appointment for 5:00 p.m. My daughter said she would take me but had some errands to run first, and she left.

I tried to clear my head. My peripheral consciousness told me that I wasn't seeing all my animals, and I was so terrified to ask about any others that I just didn't. I prayed that they were just hiding, probably out of fear. It was already starting to sink in that they had been left alone for six full weeks, with only the smallest amount of food. There wasn't even a water bowl down for them, and they had learned to live in squalor. After knowing love and comfort and affection since most of them were born, they had been left alone, often in the dark, with the stench of ammonia and filth burning their noses and eyes. It would have been futile for them to try to bathe themselves, since there was nowhere clean left to go once they bathed. Their only choice was to sleep in filth, eat what they were rationed, and try to find somewhere to defecate that wasn't already covered with feces.

~ ~ ~

Thoughts were racing through my mind. Maybe now I would be able to get some help! Maybe now I would be able to prove what was done to me! Maybe now they would believe me when I told them that my husband was sick! No one could ever see this house and these helpless animals and not know that I'd been living with horrific abuse! No one!!

I called the city police department. I was frantically trying to tell them that I had just been released from jail and had come home to horror. They seemed almost disinterested, but said they would "try" to find someone to stop by.

Officer Carl Milks eventually came up the driveway and to the back door of the family room. I had known Carl for years, and Ron and I had done legal work for him several times. I actually considered him a friend. When I saw him, I again started sobbing and was pleading with him to come in and see my entire house. He stepped inside the family room only a few feet, covered his nose and mouth, and immediately turned around to leave. I was frantically begging him to stay and let me show him the rest of the house, and he told me he "didn't need to see it." He said he had seen what he needed to see, and he didn't want to see the rest. He stood in my driveway, looking only a bit disturbed, and said, "I don't know that there's anything I can do. After all, it's Ron's house too."

Oh my God. I had just shown him proof of animal abuse and neglect, and total destruction of what had been a beautiful home, and he was telling me he wasn't going to do a damn thing about it! He got back into his police car and drove back down the driveway.

My heart sank, but only for a moment. I still had time to try to do something.

~ ~ ~

I called the newspaper. Although Marcie Schellhammer had never come back to see me at the jail—and at that time I didn't know why—I was sure they would want to know what had happened now. *Now* they would believe what I had been telling them if they saw it with their own eyes. After all, they were charged with the responsibility and obligation of reporting the news, and if this wasn't newsworthy, then nothing was. That's what I thought anyways.

I called Marty Wilder at the *Era*. I had also known Marty for years, and I was sure she would help me. My mind was again racing. I thought Marty loved animals. Yes, I was sure she loved animals. She would help me.

I heard Marty saying something like she didn't think they should get involved. I remember feeling as though someone had slapped me. I was sobbing again, and begging her to come to my house. Please, Marty, you need to see what he's done. Please, please, come here. Please come and see my house! Marty said she wasn't sure she could *spare* someone, but would see what she could do. *Oh, dear God in heaven, where are you?*

Almost amazingly, after about an hour, there was a knock on the door, and it was the *Era*'s photographer, Francie Long. She had her camera and told me Marty had asked her to stop by and take a look. *Oh, thank God! Now I know I will get some help!*

I walked Francie through every single room of my house, and she took more than a dozen pictures. She photographed piles of feces and my kitchen counters and appliances covered with filth. I remember thinking that it seemed strange that she hardly said a word and just kept walking through the house and taking pictures. She was there less than ten minutes, and I had to give her credit for having more guts than Carl Milks for walking through the house while having a really hard time breathing without choking.

I thanked her profusely for coming, and started envisioning a front-page article in the *Era* the next day with pictures of the squalor at my home. I would finally get some help! People in the community would help me now! I knew there were many animal lovers that cared as passionately for homeless animals as I did, because I had heard from many of them while I was literally fighting

City Hall the year before. People would send me cards and letters telling me that they too were trying to care for homeless and helpless animals but were afraid to let anyone know because they knew they would face the same grief I was facing. They wrote to thank me, to encourage me. I was sure these same people would help me now.

~ ~ ~

I still had some time before my daughter would pick me up to take me to the psychiatrist. My mind was still racing. *Think! Think! Who can I call? Who will help me?*

The shelter! I knew the cruelty officer well, and although most of the community saw Tony Danias as a time-wasting big mouth—and he certainly was—I knew that he loved to pat himself on the back for occasionally intervening in animal abuse situations. He fancied himself the Great Rescuer, I think, and would never let an opportunity slip by to pat himself on the back while telling you the same rescue story a dozen times over. I thought, *This is where Tony can do something good. He can certainly file charges against my husband for neglecting and abusing these animals.*

I called the shelter and left a frantic message for him, begging him to call me back. Surprisingly, he did, and he agreed to come to the house as soon as he could get there. I lived less than two miles from the shelter, so I knew it shouldn't take long. I was watching the clock, terrified of the impending 5:00 p.m. deadline, terrified of where I might be at the end of the day.

I met Tony at the door, again sobbing and trying to tell him what had happened. He had also brought his camera and immediately started taking pictures throughout the entire house. He kept muttering and mumbling to himself, "Oh my God, Ron! What were you thinking?" Over and over, he said the same thing. He was only going to photograph the downstairs, and I begged him to go upstairs to see the bedrooms and closets and the other bathroom. Although he told me he'd "seen enough," he did go up for less than a minute to take a few more pictures, and I knew that the stench was really starting to get to him. He said he "didn't need to see more," and then started to give me some lame story about how he wasn't sure there was much he could do, but he was certainly going to "look into it." *What? What does that mean? Look into what? Can't you see for yourself what has happened?*

Tony Danias promised me he would get back to me "soon." I had to believe him. I had to believe anything anyone told me, because I honestly had no choice. These people were my only hope right now. If the police and the newspaper and the SPCA couldn't help me with what had been done to my home and my animals, then I was really living in hell, right here on this godforsaken earth.

~ ~ ~

My oldest daughter came back just in time to take me to see the psychiatrist. I had known Dr. Fokstuen for many years, but had never seen him as a patient. He ushered me into his office, and I remember him being so soft-spoken and kind, offering me a chair. As I sat down, I asked him if he knew why I was there, and he told me it wasn't really clear to him. I said I had been told that I had to see a mental health professional or doctor by 5:00 p.m. that day to tell the court that I was not in need of psychiatric commitment. I spent about ten minutes trying to tell him that I had just spent the last six weeks in a jail cell because I had hit my husband, and that I wasn't able to get out or get a hearing. I told him my husband was a lawyer and that I wasn't able to find anyone to help me while I was in jail.

After I had told him as much as I could in a short amount of time, he told me that he didn't believe I was in need of commitment, and that he didn't believe I was mentally ill. He actually seemed a bit puzzled, but again was very kind to me and told me he would contact the court to advise them of his opinion. I thanked him profusely and left with my daughter, who took me back to the magistrate's office. I was again terrified, because I wasn't sure that what Dr. Fokstuen was going to say was even going to make any difference. I knew that Cercone could still harm me, especially if my husband had again asked him to, and I just prayed and prayed on the way back. I knew that Cercone could still send me back to jail, or put me in a psychiatric ward. I had absolutely no one there to advocate for me.

~ ~ ~

When I got to Cercone's office, I was told to have a seat until Stoney could see me. "Stoney" was Stoney Greenman, who was now apparently some kind of mental health counselor. I only knew Stoney from many years before, when I used to go with my girlfriends to local bars to dance and listen to bands, and he always seemed to be there, drinking a lot and hitting on young girls. Now Stoney was telling me they needed me to write some kind of statement saying that I didn't believe I was going to harm myself or anyone else, and that I was acknowledging that if I *did* feel like harming myself or others, I would contact him. I then had to put my signature on it. I remember writing that I was so happy to be going home, and that I had no intention of harming myself or anyone else. I was allowed to go home.

~ ~ ~

I asked my daughter to stop by my girlfriend's house on the way home. I knew she would help me. It didn't matter that she hadn't come to see me at the jail even once, or that she had often refused to answer my phone calls. I was sure she would help me, I was just sure. She had pets too, and we had been friends for over thirty years. Really good friends. She had introduced me to my husband and had stood up for me when we were married.

I ran up onto her porch and pounded on the door. When she answered, I threw my arms around her, sobbing. I tried to tell her about my house, and how awful it was, and how much I needed help. I begged her, "Please come help me clean! Please come help me take care of my animals!" I was so sure she would throw on her coat and boots and gladly come with me.

"I can't."

I was sure I had misheard her. "What do you mean you can't?"

"I can't. I can't handle that. I would get sick. You can stay here if you want, but I'm not going to your house."

I told her I couldn't leave my animals alone in that squalor and begged her again to come with me.

"I can't. I'm really sorry. I just can't."

She didn't ask me if I had food, or needed money, or needed anything else. She just said no.

My daughter and my son-in-law took me back to my house and said they would be able to stay for a short time to try to help me with some cleaning. I was still in absolute shock and trying to process what needed to be done. I checked the refrigerator and saw there was nothing in it that wasn't spoiled. Nothing new since before I was jailed, six weeks before. There were no cleaning supplies; there was very little cat food. My son-in-law offered to go to the store to pick up a few things. I knew they had little money, and I couldn't ask them for much, but I had come home with only change in my pocket and had no choice. They bought me a loaf of bread, a small bottle of laundry detergent, and a few other things; but there was nothing substantial. It didn't matter. I figured I would survive on whatever I could scrounge out of the cupboards; maybe there was something in cans that I could eat. What kind of meals I was going to have was the farthest thing from my mind.

I started noticing that there were more things missing than some of my animals. My microwave was gone. There was a TV/DVD player missing that my husband had bought me for Christmas the year before. There was nothing clean in the entire house. Not one clean blanket or towel or piece of clothing.

My son-in-law said he could stay for about an hour to try to do some cleaning. He got a shovel from the garage and started shoveling feces from the living and dining rooms. He took a couple of the covered litter boxes and emptied them into trash bags, the entire box of litter coming out in one huge black clump, the stench so putrid and toxic it would immediately make you start gagging and coughing, while trying to hold your breath at the same time. Unfortunately, there was no new litter box to replace it with.

Thoughts of terror just kept swirling around inside my head. Oh my God! These animals had to live this way! My sweet little babies had to climb into this squalor because they knew it was what they were supposed to do, what their instincts told them. So they just peed and peed in the same boxes for weeks, I guess, until they gave up and started using everything else. Or until the toxins overtook them and they died.

I learned much later that at least one of those sweet little animals was found dead in one of those litter boxes while I was in jail.

I cannot begin to describe for you what it is like for me to even write those words. Just thinking those words makes me wish people dead. That's the truth. My animals did absolutely *nothing* to deserve that torture, but there are humans that absolutely *did*.

~ ~ ~

My daughter and her husband said they had to get home to take care of their sons and their own work. They said they would check back with me when they had time. It seemed so strange to me that neither of them still seemed surprised or upset, and were certainly not angry or enraged or anything close to that, not even after seeing me and those animals in such a horrific place. I would realize quite a bit later why they were both so preoccupied with their own lives and my situation seemed to be nothing more than an inconvenience to them.

I was left alone with my innocent animals in total and abject squalor, with little food, with little cleaning supplies, with no money and no car. I could barely breathe the toxic air, and all I wanted to do was lie down and put my arms around as many of my furkids as possible. I had dreamed and prayed for weeks and weeks for this day. All I wanted to do was hold them and pet them and reassure them that their mama was there and I was going to take care of them like I had always done.

I washed a load of small throws and blankets and took them into the living room. I spread them out all over the little L-shaped outdoor furniture we were using for the cats. I had gotten rid of our upholstered furniture the year before when it just wasn't holding up well to the claw-sharpening and fur shedding and had replaced it with steel-coated furniture that had washable cushions. It had worked well for the cats when it was always covered with clean blankets and throws, and it was now going to work well for me. It was a hell of a lot better than a steel bunk in a jail cell! And besides, my beautiful king-sized canopy bed upstairs was pretty much destroyed, so who cared anyways?

I was so exhausted, and started sobbing again. I think I was sobbing out of both grief and relief. I was so thankful to be home. I was so thankful to not be in a cell. I was so thankful, more than anything, to be with my animals again. I lay down on the patio furniture with our throws and blankets, and some of the cats just ran over to me and jumped up beside me or crawled on top of me, purring and head-butting and crying. The stench was overwhelming, but there was nothing I could do about it. It was everywhere, and I couldn't go anywhere to get away from it. I figured if the cats had to endure it all this time, I certainly could. At least for now.

I sobbed and sobbed, cuddling and petting them. Telling them what good kids they all were, and how much Mama missed them, and how sorry I was, and how much I loved them all.

And we all fell asleep in the squalor. So thankful.

~ ~ ~

My Mother

THE NEXT DAY, I called my mother in Florida using the few minutes I had left on my cell phone. I was sure she would find a way to help me. I was sure she would be shocked and appalled when I told her what had happened, where I'd been, what my house was like. My mother had been an animal lover all her life, and I was sure she would be enraged if she heard that my animals had been left in squalor and neglected.

My mother was angry, but not at my husband. She was angry at me. My husband had talked to her while I was in jail. He had told her that her daughter was sick, a gambling addict, and that I needed to get help, so he was going to make sure I stayed in jail for a while to get the help I needed. He told my mother that he was so worried about me, and that he would do anything he could to help me get better. He knew that jail was the "best" place for me right now, and my mother told him that she understood, that she appreciated what he was going through and what he was doing for me. She felt very sorry for him.

I again remembered my husband's words: "Who do you think they're going to believe? *You* or *me*?"

I sobbed and sobbed and begged my mother to help me, to *believe* me. She said she wouldn't do anything to help me because I needed to get help. I told her I had prescriptions for blood pressure medications that I couldn't pick up at the pharmacy because I had no money, and she told me the best she could do was to send me my Christmas gift early and I could use that. She sent me a check for $100 a few days later, and I walked to town in the snow to cash it and pick up my medications.

My mother just kept telling me I was sick, and that she felt so sorry for my husband. I cried and pleaded with her to listen to me, and she told me she didn't want to hear it.

Looking back, I realized how consistent my mother was. When I was married to an alcoholic, he was always so charming and personable to my mother, and she liked him much more than she liked me. She once told him she felt I was a millstone around his neck and that I was holding him back. I'm not sure from what, but I wasn't going to change her mind.

~ ~ ~

A Little Help

LATER IN THE day, I had a couple of visitors. The mayor of our city had been an acquaintance of ours for years, and we frequently ate at his wife's Texas Hots restaurant. He stopped by with his wife and her father and brought me a meal and a small amount of cleaning supplies. The mayor and his father-in-law spent a couple of hours trying to do a little cleaning, but I could tell it was way too overwhelming for them too. His wife brought me a small air purifier that she got from a friend of hers, and I couldn't thank them enough. I was sure that somehow they would help me beyond that day, and I started to get hopeful again. I was so thankful that they had seen the devastation and was sure they wouldn't just leave us in it. I was also sure that through their connections, they would get the word out and I would get a lot more help. And maybe he could even help me get my husband prosecuted for animal abuse and neglect, since we lived within the city limits.

That turned out to be wishful thinking. As I found out much later, so many people didn't want to get involved, and many others saw my husband as a nice guy that must have had some good reason for what he had done.

Another "friend," the wife of a pastor who had counseled us a couple of times, stopped by with a small package of sliced ham, some crackers, and fruit. Enough that I could make it last more than a day if I rationed carefully. I was in tears when I saw her because, again, I was so hopeful that her coming to see me was some indication that she and her husband would help me and my animals. But after talking to her for a few minutes, I knew it wasn't going to be that way. I had written to the pastor while I was in jail, begging him to go see my husband and convince him to get me out and let me go home. I had told him how afraid I was of what would happen to my animals. He never responded. That day his wife told me that the reason he didn't respond to me was because he didn't really think it was appropriate for him to get involved when he considered us both to be "friends" of his. She looked at me, very sincerely, and said, "I'm sure you understand his position." And my heart sank.

No! I could *not* understand that position. If any friend of mine ever wrote to me or called me and asked me for help and said they were locked up and they had animals to care for that would die if they couldn't care for them, *no!* I would not ignore them, and I would not tell them "I don't want to get involved." At the very least, I would have done whatever I could do to try to care for the animals and get others to help.

These people said they were Christians, led a small church, and were telling me that they didn't want to get involved because my husband and I were both friends of theirs. That was so painful for me to hear. My husband was driving around in my car, chasing other women, drinking seven days a week, eating in restaurants and causing horrific harm to our animals, and I was in a cell block. My "friends" didn't want to be seen as showing favoritism to one of us, so they just stayed away.

If you have friends in hell, I'm pretty sure they're just like that.

~ ~ ~

When I was released from the jail, I was still suffering from respiratory infection, and now was faced with living in a house that was filled with toxic air and surfaces. I learned to move from one area to another, one room to another, cleaning small areas as I had supplies and strength. I would move the small air purifier from one area to another while I worked, trying to breathe as much "clean" air as I could, stepping outside often to get fresh air, and sleeping with the air purifier next to my head. It took me three weeks to get most of the rooms cleaned, a few square feet at a time. During that time, I got much sicker than I was when I came home, my throat was always sore and my voice got very hoarse. But I was just so thankful to be home and to be caring for my furkids again.

~ ~ ~

Welfare

—⋯➤❖◀⋯—

I HAD ALWAYS known that Pennsylvania was one of the easiest states in which to get lots of public assistance benefits. My husband had represented so many people, especially young people, that were getting substantial monthly cash benefits, food stamps, rent subsidies, free medical care and prescriptions, and even money to buy a used car. I was hopeful that they would somehow be able to help me, because I literally had no place else to turn.

I had worked most of my adult life and had paid taxes like everyone else that worked. I tried to tell myself that it was okay to be asking for help when I really had no other options. Going to the welfare office was one of the most humiliating experiences I've ever had, and it wasn't because I had to ask for help. It was because I was treated as though I was trying to cheat the system, and they didn't believe a word I told them.

I sat in the waiting area every time I went there for well over an hour, sometimes more than two hours. I watched dozens of very young people come in with babies and very young children, many of them dirty with uncombed hair and dirty clothing. They would play with their cell phones while their babies crawled around on the filthy floor and didn't flinch or pay much attention. I overheard conversations from these same people that made it clear that they expected even more than they were getting for free and were disgusted that they had to go out of their way to get something for free. They complained about everything and ignored their children.

When I was finally able to talk to someone, I was given a laundry list of things I had to provide them to prove that I had nothing. Because I had made money earlier that year on a house flip, they told me they had to impute that money to a twelve-month period, so I would not be eligible for any cash assistance until the year was up, the next July. It was only December!

I applied for financial assistance to buy a used vehicle since my husband had taken my car. I jumped through their hoops and one afternoon got a call from the assistance office telling me that they believed I was trying to defraud them. They said they had received a "tip" that I had a nice vehicle parked in my yard, so I *must* have been lying when I said I didn't have one!

The "nice vehicle" that was parked in my backyard in two feet of snow was my husband's pickup truck. He had removed the plates from it so I couldn't drive it and had canceled the insurance. I told them my husband had taken my car and I had no access to it, but they didn't believe me. I got nothing from them for a vehicle.

I was stunned. My daughter had a friend whose husband said he had learned to work the system and would find some part-time job, go to the welfare office to get money for a vehicle, buy a vehicle, and then quit the job shortly after that. He would wait a year and do the same thing over again. And over again. They never stopped giving him money for a car, and yet they would routinely get between $3,000 and $5,000 every year from the earned income tax credit because he had worked something during the year, but not enough.

I was finally able to get $159 in food stamps, and because my friend always told me she had no money, I would take her with me to Walmart and let her fill her cart, using up a substantial portion of my balance.

The last time I went to the welfare office, I left sobbing. I told them I had worked all my life and had always paid taxes, and I was now in a desperate situation and I couldn't believe I was being treated like some kind of lowlife. What I finally realized was that my biggest problem—to them—was that I had worked most of my life. I just gave up.

My Best Friend

I WAS REALLY hurt that one of my oldest and best friends had never visited me in jail, and wouldn't help me after I got home

I knew that she didn't have much time for me anymore if I couldn't take her to the casino, and since I never had money for anything after being released from jail, I had become kind of a nuisance to her. When my husband would be generous enough to buy some cases of cat food for the furkids, for a time he was taking them to my friend's house and leaving them there for me to pick up. One evening, when I went to pick up the cat food, my friend told me she wanted to talk to me about something. She got out a big white envelope and told me that my husband had left it with her, asking her to take a look at it and then have a talk with me.

In the envelope was a seven-page proposal for a divorce settlement. It had been written by my husband and typed by my own daughter, who was still working for him. His proposal was that I would essentially give him everything, not make a claim against him for anything more than a small pittance he would give me biweekly to take care of the animals, and that I would agree to a divorce. Oh yeah, and he was insisting that I give him two of the cats. He said they were his "favorites." I guess those would be the favorites that he left in squalor and contamination for six weeks while they nearly starved to death and were desperately alone. They would be the favorites that he would regularly threaten to have euthanized. They would be the favorites that he intentionally abused and neglected.

I read his proposal at my friend's house, and I almost threw up. My head and my heart were pounding, and I was shaking all over. I looked at my friend and said, "He's got to be kidding." And my best friend said, very calmly, "Cathy, I think you should sign it. You need to put this behind you and move on with your life."

I thought my heart actually stopped for a few seconds. I could not believe this was my best friend saying these words.

I got the cases of cat food into my borrowed truck and went home, and I sobbed.

The (Literal) Rapist

I GATHERED TOGETHER every piece of jewelry I owned. My wedding ring, engagement ring, pearl ring, two 14k gold chains, and a piece of heirloom jewelry my mother had given me. I took all my jewelry to a gold buyer and got $400 for it. I then went to the cable company and paid for a month's worth of phone, TV, and Internet. I bought groceries and cat food and cleaning supplies. I would have happily sold my husband's wedding ring if he hadn't thrown it in the garbage months before. I was so angry that I hadn't fished it out of the garbage can before I put it out to be picked up. I guess I never figured I'd need it so desperately one day.

The whole time I was going through hell and anguish, I would often think about the rapist. *My* rapist. The pervert who had stolen so much from me. I always figured he got away with it, and always wished I'd someday find out he died some horrible death at a young age.

When I was able to get my Internet and phone turned back on, I knew it would most likely be only for a short time. I had no idea where I was going to get any more money to pay for another month of service, so I figured I'd better do everything and anything online that I possibly could.

One very cold winter afternoon, I decided to type in the rapist's name. Oh my God! I couldn't believe what I found. There was his name, his address, his age, his city, and an aerial view of his house. He was living in West Virginia, and the information said he was married. As I did a further Google search, I found where he was working—for a State of West Virginia agency. I knew that he would have had to pass a background check for that job. I was sure of that. So I was also sure he never mentioned that he had once raped a child. Or was it just once?

By this time, I was so used to living in either fear or pain that I just told myself, *You damn well better do this now, while you have the opportunity and nothing much left to lose!* And I picked up the phone and called his number.

It was a weekend, so I was hoping he would be home. The phone rang, and my heart pounded so hard I could hear it in both ears. I could barely breathe.

A woman answered the phone. "Hello?"

"May I speak to Conrad Bramlee, please?"

"He's busy. He can't come to the phone right now. Who is this?"

"You just tell your husband that he raped me when I was a child, and I think he'll make time to talk to me."

"What? What did you say?"

And I repeated what I said.

"Just a minute!" And I heard her yelling at the top of her lungs for him to come to the phone.

Conrad decided to take the phone from her. "Hello? Who's this?"

"Well, Conrad, my name is Cathy, and I used to live on South Avenue in Bradford, Pennsylvania, and when I was nine years old, you grabbed me off the street and took me into your house, and you raped me. Remember me now?"

I guess Conrad must have had a cat that got his tongue for a few minutes, because I think I heard him starting to have a stroke or something interesting like that. I think I actually would have enjoyed hearing his wife come to the phone and tell me her husband just dropped dead. (Yes, you're right, that's not a very Christian attitude, but that's just how I felt.)

I spent the next five minutes or so giving Conrad every detail I could remember about the rape, and then the follow-up visit with my parents while I was again victimized by both his parents and mine making me sit in the same room with him to try to explain what he had done, all the while not understanding a damn thing and just being abjectly terrified.

I told the rapist how I could still recall every single sickening detail of what he had done to me, and how he had damaged my heart and soul since I was a little girl.

When I was done walking him down memory lane, I heard him say, "Well, that's not exactly how I remember it." And I said, "Maybe that's because you did it more than once. Maybe you did it to other girls." Quiet. He said nothing. I said "You *did*. You did it more than just to me, didn't you?" And then I heard him meekly say, "No." And I said, "You're a damn liar, and we both know it." He said nothing. I knew a lot about my husband's former clients who had admitted to sexually abusing children, and there was *no one* who ever did it *once*. Not one! And I knew Conrad probably spent much of his early life molesting children when he had the chance, and for all I knew, he'd been doing it all his life. As long as they don't go to jail or get seriously punished or have serious consequences, they never, ever stop. I had done a rather extensive Google search on Conrad and found there were no criminal proceedings against him ever. So he either stopped at me, or he just never got caught. I'd bet the bank on the latter.

For days, after my phone conversation with the rapist, I was physically sick to my stomach. I've learned that suffering from posttraumatic stress issues your entire life is common. All you have to do is go back there in your mind, and you're just *there*, physically, mentally, and emotionally. It's like it's all happening again, in real time, right now.

Every time I see a news story about another child being victimized in any way, it just breaks my heart for them. I know they'll never be really over it no matter how many years go by, because it just damages their very being, even their very soul, and it can haunt them in their nightmares or in the middle of the day.

After my phone conversation with the rapist, I did online research for about a week and spoke to many people in different states who ran counseling centers or who were advocates for victims of childhood sexual abuse. I was hoping against hope that there would be some way I could still have the rapist charged and have to answer.

For the prior forty-six years, I never knew where he was. I had tried to find him online when I first got a computer and Internet service, but the only thing I ever found was his mother's obituary. I thought that maybe there was some legal loophole that would let me file charges now since I could never find him. What I found was that Delaware was the only state in the country that actually had a law that would allow you to prosecute a child rapist regardless of how many years had passed. I was told that there were many advocates trying to get the laws changed in other states, but it was going to take a long time. And it would never happen soon enough to help me.

I honestly hope that Conrad's wife beat him senseless after my phone call, and that's just the truth.

December 20
Spousal Support Hearing

So exhausted and getting sicker, I was really trying to be hopeful that I was finally going to get some help. I knew that Debbie Babcox had long been the Family Law Master, and I knew she was a friend and colleague of my husband's. I still held out hope that either she would be at least a little bit fair to me, or that she would have been replaced by the court because there would definitely be a conflict of interest, and there was little possibility that she would, or could, be fair.

Because I had no vehicle and no money, Cheryl had tried to help me get there by calling people from the jail. I got a call from someone—I can't even remember who now—saying that a woman who had a jail ministry would give me a ride to the courthouse. When she picked me up, I discovered she was someone I'd known for years, but only as an acquaintance.

It was a real blizzard that day, and the roads were horrible. The only way to get to the courthouse was over steep hills and winding roads, and I would have been terrified if I didn't know how important it was to get some help for myself and the animals. I prayed the whole way and tried to be hopeful.

She picked me up at the bottom of my driveway and did scare the hell out of me the entire trip. I was sure we'd go off the road at some point, but I've learned to believe that angels are always with me when I travel, and I'm sure they were that day. The snowfall was nearly blinding, and the accumulation was deep, even on the roadways, but we made it.

I had put together copies of excerpts from my husband's online posts, from the porn addiction website. I had carefully chosen the posts where he specifically wrote that he had "totally destroyed" our marriage, that he was "sick," that I had suffered greatly because of him, and that I had stood by him for nineteen years while he put me through hell.

I waited in the hallway outside the main courtroom and saw both my husband and his lawyer/friend Greg walk past me several times, always in the direction of the hearing room, where Debbie would hold the hearings. I was sure they were talking to her beforehand. I knew how it worked. I had known for years how it worked. If Debbie knew someone personally who was involved in any kind of dispute over which she presided, you could bet the bank that she would rule in their favor. I knew how that worked too.

When I was finally called in for the hearing, there she was, sitting behind her desk. I was still praying, hoping that since she was a woman, she would at least listen to me, and maybe sympathize with me a little when I told her what I had been going through for years.

Greg and my husband sat across the table from me, and we were sworn in. His turn first. Greg told Debbie what an awful, criminal, abusive wife I had been. He told her I had taken money from my husband's bank account, that I had assaulted him, that I had just been released from jail. Greg questioned Ron, and he questioned me. I answered every question truthfully, and my husband repeatedly lied, under oath. It wasn't the first time he'd lied under oath.

I looked at my own husband across that table. I had no idea who he was. This was a man who looked back at me with a blank stare. I still had the grown-out, graying hair, and I had lost a lot of weight. I had scrounged up something to wear that wasn't destroyed to wear to court, and he was in dress clothes, like his lawyer. Just like before, in the PFA hearing, I looked like death warmed over, he looked like a professional.

When Greg was done presenting my husband's "case", I was told it was my turn. I was allowed to question my husband. I asked him straightforward questions about the threats and abuse, and he denied every single thing. I heard him tell Debbie he would admit he "hadn't always been a great husband," and looked as though he wanted a pat on the back for saying it. Typical abuser.

When I started to ask him about his pornography and other addictions, Debbie cut me off. She told me she didn't want to hear it. She said, "Mrs. Langella, I've heard enough."

I heard Debbie say that my husband had "proven" that I was not entitled to *any* support from him because I was the one who had harmed *him*. I took my big envelope full of excerpts from his porn addiction posts and tried to hand it to her. She put her hand up to me, palm first, and said, "Mrs. Langella, I'm not interested in anything you have to show me."

I thought I would pass out. *Oh no! This can't happen! I have to have help to take care of our animals!* I asked her why *she* was the one that was hearing my petition for support. I told her she obviously wasn't capable of being impartial, and she very calmly said, "Are you asking me to recuse myself from this case?" I said yes, I was, and that she never should have heard it in the first place.

She said fine, she would ask that someone else be appointed to hear the matter, and the hearing was over. After I'd waited months and after I'd literally risked my life to get there.

It had been a waste of everything. Time, stress, anxiety, hope, tears, everything. A waste.

~ ~ ~

I was dropped off at home in a daze. I knew it was only four days until Christmas Eve, always my favorite day of the year my entire life. I was alone, but not really alone. I had unconditional love from my animals, and I thought that God might still be looking in on me from somewhere. I was still shaking my fist at him and begging him to tell me why he was allowing these things to happen to me. So many of my rescues were very sick, but all of them were very happy to see me and trying to crowd each other out for a turn on my lap or a snuggle up against me.

That day I decided that we were going to have our own Christmas, and no one was going to take it away from us. At least not now. There was a real sense of peace and quiet in my once-beautiful big house full of ruined furniture and traces of the stench from animal waste. I knew that I must have at least a few boxes of Christmas decorations packed away in the basement, and started telling my furkids out loud, "Mama's going to decorate the house for you guys, and we're going to have Christmas!"

Yep, I'm sure I sounded like a real nutcase. Too bad. It was how I was going to survive that day.

I not only found a few boxes of ornaments and lights that I'd saved from past Christmases, but I realized there was a big artificial tree in a box. Without using enough common sense to realize I could have taken it out of the box in pieces to get it up the stairs, I pushed and pulled and lugged the huge box up the basement stairs with the whole tree inside. I was able to assemble it enough to make it look like a tree, and after covering it with tons of ornaments and lights, I thought it was the most beautiful thing I'd seen in a long time. It stood in the corner of the living room, next to the fireplace and mantel that I would always decorate with garlands and lights and wonderful decorations. Not this year, though. This year I had just enough energy to put up a scraggly fake tree and think it looked beautiful. I left it lit for weeks until the lights burned out. It made my living room the greatest place to curl up with my furkids and listen to music with just the Christmas lights on.

It was a prayer answered. I had prayed and prayed that I would be home with my rescues for Christmastime, and I was.

Christmas Eve 2007

MY HUSBAND CALLED my cell phone and left a message that he was going to drop off some cat food. He said he'd leave it on the porch, but he didn't show up. I knew he'd be drinking, and that was probably why. When I first started dating my husband, he told me that he believed he was "on the verge" of becoming an alcoholic, and said he wanted us to have a good marriage, and that he thought his drinking might cause problems, so he actually quit. The last time he'd had a drink was at a county bar meeting at a local hotel just after we were married, and he had gone nearly twenty years without a drink. But I had been told that he started drinking again the night he had me sent to jail, and that started just another daily, dangerous habit. Dangerous for him, but much more so for me and my rescues.

~ ~ ~

I had another unexpected visitor instead. Tony Danias, the cruelty officer from the SPCA. He brought me a few dented cans of cat food and half a bag of cat litter he'd actually taken from the shelter. I knew Tony wasn't going to pay for anything himself, or give us anything out of his own pocket. That wasn't Tony.

I had been calling Tony regularly and leaving messages for him. I wanted to know what he was going to do about filing charges against my husband for animal abuse and neglect. After all, he had seen everything with his own eyes, and had taken pictures of the squalor himself.

True to form, Tony was his cowardly self. Big mouth, big talker, big fake. He told me he had been investigating what I said my husband had done. I started yelling at him and asking him what the hell he meant by "investigating." He had seen everything for himself! He told me even if he did feel that filing charges were appropriate, there was a "problem" getting them filed. He said he would have to talk to Dom (Cercone) and "get him to agree" that it was okay for him to file the charges in Cercone's office. We lived in the city, and Cercone's jurisdiction was in the city.

Pathetic, cowardly Tony then said, "You know, Cathy, I've talked to two different cruelty officers from other counties, and they both told me I'd be crazy to file charges against a lawyer."

I'm pretty sure my yelling turned into screaming. This was a man being paid by the SPCA to be a cruelty officer, and he was telling me, to my face, that he was afraid of what my husband might do to him because he was a lawyer. By now I was crying, and Tony promised that he would still try to do something. Right.

~ ~ ~

A couple of months later, I saw Tony in the parking lot of my veterinarian's office and pulled in beside him. I walked up to him, interrupting his conversation with the vet and got in his face. I asked him to explain to me just exactly *what* he had done so far, and how his "investigation" was coming along.

Pathetic, cowardly Tony looked me straight in the eye and said, "Cathy, you know, I *never* saw no dead cats."

I started sobbing and screaming at him. "What are you talking about? You saw my house! You saw the squalor and devastation! You know I had terribly sick animals! You could barely breathe in there!"

Pathetic, cowardly Tony said the most horrific thing he could have ever said to me: "Cathy, you don't care about no cats. You just care about yourself. This was always just about you. This was always just about Cathy."

I screamed, "You son of a bitch!" And I left.

My husband's now-prophetic words again echoed through my pounding head. *Who do you think they're going to believe, you or me?*

January 2008

A couple of weeks after Christmas, I spoke to Marcie Schellhammer at the newspaper again. I asked her why she never came back to see me in jail.

Marcie told me she couldn't. I asked her what she meant she couldn't. She said she wasn't allowed to go back to see me. Then she very matter-of-factly told me that the paper had been "threatened with a lawsuit" if they printed anything about my husband, or about what had happened to me.

Marcie told me that John Egbert, chairman of the McKean County Board of Commissioners, had personally visited the newspaper's office and had *warned* them not to print anything that had anything to do with my husband. You see, John Egbert was really my husband's employer as one of the county commissioners. By now, John Egbert knew about my husband's porn addictions, knew that I'd been kept in jail without a hearing and without bail, and knew an awful lot of what had been going on. Every time I had written a letter to the court, to the newspaper, or to any government agency, either from jail or from home, I had copied the Board of Commissioners, so John Egbert knew a lot, and he had enough power to be able to stop the newspaper from printing a thing. Actually, they didn't need much persuasion.

Marcie also seemed to honestly take delight in telling me some news I hadn't heard. She asked me if I knew my husband had been in an accident. I didn't. She told me he had wrecked his car, and she wasn't sure if he'd been hurt. Sometime after Christmas, she said, but couldn't remember exactly when.

The car he would have been driving, and would have "wrecked," would have been mine. I guess I didn't have a right to know, and although there would have been an accident report, and the police would have known everything that had been going on with us, no one ever notified me. I would later find out that the police didn't think I had a right to my own car anyways, so no big deal.

Super Bowl Sunday 2008
(Part 1)

I was desperately hoping I would have another chance to get my car back. I had been interviewed at an animal shelter across the New York State line and had been asked when I could start on a trial basis. My time was running out to be able to try the job. My car was the only reliable transportation I had, and I couldn't get my own car away from my husband.

Since my husband had started drinking again, it was a sure bet that he'd be drinking at a bar for the Super Bowl. His apartment was within walking distance from several bars, so I drove past the bars and his apartment to see if I could locate my car. I had borrowed my son-in-law's very old, very beat-up truck.

After driving past a couple of the bars he frequented, I spotted my car behind his apartment in an alleyway. There was no one around. No neighbors, no traffic. It was very quiet.

I parked my son-in-law's truck on the street. I ran down the alleyway and opened the car door with my key.

There was a "Club" locked on the steering wheel. My heart sank, and my head was spinning. I knew I didn't have a lot of time to waste, because he would be drinking at a bar close by. I tried desperately to remove the Club, but of course, I couldn't. Before I went back to the truck, I decided that there was no way he was going to drive *my* car after he'd been drinking all day, so I opened the hood and started removing the air filter. I figured if I removed a few parts from the engine, he couldn't start it, and would at least have to sober up before he could drive it again.

Seemingly out of nowhere, I had company. I noticed someone with a dog standing between two houses, watching me. It was Barb, Greg's secretary. I matter-of-factly said to her, "If I can't drive my own car, he isn't going to drive it either." And I went back to removing the parts.

Literally, within a few *minutes*, as I was closing the hood, I started back up the alleyway and saw my husband walking toward me. He was smiling, and he had his phone up to his ear. It wasn't the kind of smile you'd see on a normal person. I knew well my husband's sickness, and knew well his sick smiles.

Barb had called him when she saw me with my own car, and he was only minutes away.

He said, "Cathy, what are you doing? You know you're going back to jail, don't you?" And he kept smiling while he called the police in front of me.

I just ran through the snow, as fast as I could possibly move, back to the truck, my heart pounding, barely able to breathe, terrified of what was going to happen next. I drove home as fast as I could.

When I got home, I just sobbed, and again screamed at God, asking him why he was allowing all of this to happen. *Please tell me! Why are you letting this man do these things? Why are you allowing this?*

I was again absolutely terror-stricken that my husband was going to find another way to put me back in a cell, and that the rest of my rescues would be killed or suffer even more than they already had.

~ ~ ~

Within a few days of Super Bowl Sunday, I received a packet of court documents from the attorney general Tom Corbett's Office. (Tom Corbett went on to become governor of Pennsylvania.) Based upon information given to them by Ron, the AG's office in Pittsburgh had filed a petition with the court asking that my bail be revoked and that I be sent back to jail. They said I had violated the terms of my bail because I had gone near my husband. *But I had not!* I had gone to a back alley driveway while he was in a bar blocks away, and I had only tried to get my *own* car! The petition also alleged that I had "vandalized" my husband's property! It was my car!! I had removed some parts from the air filter to keep him from driving it drunk!

His words again echoed in my head. *Cathy, who do you think they're going to believe? You or me?*

Barb

I HAD KNOWN Barb for nearly twenty years, but only as someone that had once been Ron and Greg's secretary, and had worked solely for Greg for many years. She was never friendly, was always very standoffish and a bit arrogant, but that always seemed to go with the territory in the legal community. When I first met her, I was told that her new husband was a lawyer she had started dating while he was married with young children. I was told she was responsible for the breakup of his family and marriage, and that she was a party girl who loved male attention. A few years after I met them, her lawyer husband died from complications after surgery. I learned that there was quite a dispute over who would get what money after the hospital and/or doctors were sued.

For quite some time, Barb was dating and/or living with Chris Hauser. Even after they broke up, she continued to live in one of his rental apartments, which is why it was so handy for her to be able to call the police when I attempted to retrieve my car from the alleyway.

Barb and Greg, her boss, seemed to have a real love/hate relationship. They were always snapping at each other. It was apparent to me that she didn't have much respect for Greg, since I would often overhear her telling his clients about him, usually in a derogatory manner. One afternoon, while I was standing by her desk, waiting for her to get off the phone, I heard her tell a client, "Greg told you that and you *believed* him?" Another time, I heard her say "If you told Greg something two weeks ago, you can't possibly expect him to remember it now!"

I think Barb and Greg absolutely deserve each other. Both extremely self-serving, self-absorbed users, who only see other people as a means to an end.

Last I knew, Barb was having an affair with another married man. I was told he lived out of the area, and his wife didn't know about her.

Trying to Get Help

I HAD WRITTEN to Judge Cleland and Judge Yoder and the commissioners and the newspaper and had begged all of them—*any of them*—for help. Not just for myself, but for my animals. I often had absolutely no money at all and had dozens of animals to feed and care for. I was going to go back to jail if I even tried to contact my husband, even through a third party, so that wasn't even an option. I knew my rescues would all be dead if I was taken away from them again.

It was the middle of winter, and I often didn't have a phone, often didn't have a way to even get to the store if I had any money. I was trying not to spend every waking moment crying and panicking, and was always trying to think of ways to get help. I remember vividly one day being so terrified that my animals were going to starve to death. I had absolutely no food left for them, no money, and I was truly desperate. I called anyone and everyone that I could think of—at least anyone whose phone number I could remember—and left hysterical, sobbing messages. "Please help me! I have no food left for my animals! Please, if there is anything at all you can do, please help me!"

One time when I had been able to get some paper for my printer, I typed up a letter addressed to no one in particular and, borrowing my son-in-law's beater truck, drove it around town in a blizzard to half a dozen churches and the Salvation Army and left it in mail slots. I offered to trade my piano or just about anything I had left for food and cleaning supplies and cat litter.

My water heater blew up and flooded my basement one bitter cold day, and I could not call my husband to get it fixed, or I was going back to jail. I called the police department and told Mike Ward that I desperately needed to get it fixed because I couldn't clean anything without hot water, and was afraid we'd end up back in squalor. Hours later, Mike Ward called me back and told me he had spoken to my husband. He said, "He says he's not spending any more money on that house since it's going back to the bank, so you'll have to figure out something else." I just started sobbing again and asked him what I was supposed to do, and he basically told me it wasn't his problem.

I decided to try another way to get the attention of *anyone,* and went into my basement and found leftover pieces of luan, particleboard and plywood—anything I could write on—and used black paint and markers and made the biggest signs I could make. I tried to tell my story on the boards and kept writing, "Please help me!" I nailed them all to the front of my house, on my big front porch. When I ran out of room and signs, I used the black paint and wrote more pleading messages on the siding and trim on the porch. I wrote about the county's corruption and my husband's abuse and my animals being left to die.

A few days after I put the signs up, a man across the street told me that the police had pulled up in front of my house and had taken pictures. I never heard why, and I don't know what they were going to use them for, unless it was to help my husband try to prove, again, that I was crazy.

Looking back, I know now it was truly God's grace that kept me from literally going mad.

~ ~ ~

On many other desperate days, I would drag things out of my garage or basement, whatever I could carry myself, and put it out on the front lawn. The snow was so deep sometimes, and I would pull ladders, our snowblower, an air conditioner, and anything at all I thought I might be able to get a few dollars for, tripping and falling in the snow many times, and put homemade signs on everything, asking for $25 or $30. I had no money to place ads, and often had no Internet, so this was about all I could think of. I would hear a knock at the door and never know if I should be terrified it was someone coming to harm me, or thankful that it was just someone who wanted to buy something from me. Anytime I would get any money at all, I would either walk to town or take a bus and get as many cans of cat food or rolls of paper towels that I could afford, and could carry, and lug them home. I remember so well how good it felt when I was finally back home and knew I could feed my rescues for another couple of days.

One True Friend

THERE *WAS* ONE person—only one—who did not totally abandon me. I had a longtime friend that I had known well from my days on the local board of the SPCA, and from our many conversations about our common love for animals, especially homeless and abandoned animals. He had been rescuing cats and kittens for many more years than I had, and he had a heart of gold. He was my inspiration early on in my rescuing years, as he had shown me the little "cabin" in his backyard that he had converted into a heated shelter for his rescues. I had known him, but not that well, since our high school days, and he had been a local businessman for many years. He had played guitar in a local band on weekends since I'd known him, and I knew that he had used the money he made from his part-time love of music to make things better for his full-time love, his rescues.

To this day, I admire him more than anyone I've ever known. He went out of his way to help me and my rescues when everyone else had turned their backs, and never once questioned me or treated me like I was some kind of criminal, or loser, or nuts. He just treated me like a true friend. What a blessing he was.

When we were on the board of the shelter, we both volunteered for rabies clinics and painting the dog kennels and trying to do what we could to make it better. I had gone there dozens of times to clean or take supplies, and one Christmas bought them a big artificial tree and tons of lights and ornaments to try to make the place more inviting for prospective adopters. Over one Fourth of July weekend, when the shelter was closed and no one was around, in ninety-degree heat, I spent hours weeding and cleaning up outside, planting flowers and hanging baskets. I always did it for the animals. My heart broke for every single one of them every time I had to look in a cage at a terrified, lonely cat, or see the big dogs no one wanted just begging for a new mama or daddy. I just wanted them to have homes, and there were never enough.

~ ~ ~

After being home from jail only a short time, this friend knocked on my front door in the middle of a snowstorm. I hadn't seen or talked to him in months and didn't even know if he knew what had been going on. I learned that he had read in the newspaper that I had been in jail. He told me to get in his car and he took me to Walmart, where he bought me a cartful of groceries and gave me cash to buy some antibiotics for my sickest cats from our vet. He had already brought medications that he used for his own rescues and helped me give some of them injections.

I was so grateful to him that I could barely speak. I just cried, and thanked him profusely. And I was so ashamed of my husband, so much more than I already was. Several times after that day he would leave huge tubs of cat litter, cleaning supplies and cat food on my front porch without even letting me know he was coming. Twice more he bought me groceries when I had nothing. He was truly a Guardian Angel to me and my furkids so many times.

This kind man told me he had gone to my husband several times while I was incarcerated and had offered to help with our rescues while I wasn't there. He offered to treat the ones that were sick and help clean the place up. He didn't ask any questions; he just wanted to help.

My husband refused him *every* time.

Well, my husband didn't refuse all his offers of help. My friend told me that my husband took over $400 in cash from him and promised him he would spend it all on our animals. My husband did not need money to care for our animals. He had plenty. He was eating in restaurants and drinking in bars every day. He was going on "shopping trips" and once took his buddy Greg to Red Lobster, paying $80 for their dinners. He bought himself an entire new wardrobe of dress clothes and all kinds of things he didn't need.

And yet he took over $400 from my animal-loving, very-hardworking friend, and it made me so sick when I found out. And so ashamed.

Another Court Hearing–Divorce

A HEARING ON the divorce complaint my husband had filed was actually scheduled sooner than a hearing on my emergency petition for spousal support, which I had filed months before. A senior judge from Clarion County, Richard Saxton, was appointed to oversee the case. I was just a little hopeful that he would be fairer and more impartial than anyone from McKean County.

Days before the hearing I was trying to do everything I could to prepare for what I thought would be my testimony. I called Francie Long at the *Bradford Era* and asked her how I could get copies of the photographs she had taken in my house—the photographs of the squalor and destruction she had personally seen.

Francie told me she had been told to destroy the pictures. She said she had been told there "*isn't* going to be a story" and she was to destroy the pictures.

Francie's orders could have only come from one of two people. Either Marty Wilder had given her those orders, or John Satterwhite himself had ordered her to do it. No one else had the authority at the *Era* to give orders to destroy photos of animal abuse and neglect. No one but Marty or John Satterwhite.

~ ~ ~

I called Tony Danias, the "cruelty officer" at the McKean County SPCA. *The same Tony that had told me he didn't dare file charges against my husband for animal cruelty because my husband was a lawyer.*

Like Francie, Tony Danias told me "I don't have no pictures." He said he didn't think he needed to save them and so he had deleted them.

~ ~ ~

I called Mike Ward at the city police station and left several messages for him. I told him I needed him to testify at the divorce hearing about what he knew. I would never hear back from Mike Ward, and the next time I ran into him at the courthouse, he told me that he had been having problems with his voice mail and he didn't know I'd tried to reach him.

Yeah, right.

And so I went to my hearing with absolutely nothing to support my contention that my husband was very sick and had abused and neglected our rescues. Depending on your point of view, I guess it didn't matter, because I wasn't going to be allowed to testify anyways.

~ ~ ~

The hearing was held in the large courtroom, which was unusual for divorce hearings. Most of the people in the courtroom–again–were either friends, colleagues, or both, of my husband's. When I tried to ask the judge why my petition for spousal support had not yet been heard, he started yelling at me in open court, telling me that he was going to "take care of everything" in one hearing. He was going to handle the divorce case and my petition for support at the same time. My hope was fading fast, but I hadn't given up completely—yet.

I should have known better. I was given a copy of an "income and expense statement" that had been prepared by my husband and provided to the court. It was nothing more than about ten lines of fantasy. He said he hardly had any income, and that his expenses to run the office were more than twice what he took in. He showed that he was making a substantial mortgage payment on the office building, and I knew he hadn't made any mortgage payments in a long time, either on our home or the office.

I tried to tell the judge that the information my husband had given the court was bogus, and the judge told me he had no reason not to believe his numbers. *Really?*

Then Judge Saxton gave me what he thought was fair. He said that based upon my husband's representations to the court, he would award me $350 every two weeks in spousal support–$175 a week. That was exactly what we were spending on our rescues for food, litter, and cleaning supplies. The judge then went on to explain that he was *imputing* what I could *potentially* make if I were working a full-time job in fashioning his award of $175 a week. He did not want to hear that my husband had taken my car and that I had no ability to pursue any full-time work without it.

Honestly, Judge Saxton didn't want to hear a damn thing I had to say. He had made up his mind before he even met me and, like Debbie Babcox before him, was not going to let anything I had to say sway him or convince him that he was wrong. Therefore, he had no reason to take testimony from me. I was doomed before I got there. I was doomed before I even filed the paperwork asking for support.

Reconciliation?

I HAD TRIED everything I could think of to save my home and find answers for my animals and me. I had called the bank that held our mortgage and had talked to the bank's president, Marty Digel. I had received notice of the scheduling of the sheriff's sale for my house and had no idea what was going to happen to us.

I was sobbing and begging Marty to please tell me what they were going to do, what was going to happen. In Marty's typical condescending, mocking voice, he said, "Well, Cathy, I guess you'll just have to leave." And I asked, "But what will happen to my animals?"

Marty just continued on in his sing-song condescension and said, "Well, I guess we'll have to call the shelter or the police, and they'll just have to put them out in the middle of the street with you."

I was hysterical, and he hung up.

I started making phone calls to the courthouse. I talked to the judges' secretaries and the court administrator. I was so panicked and sobbing and could barely speak. I just kept saying "Why isn't anyone helping me? Why are you all protecting my husband?"

They told me they were sorry, and "nothing we can do" and hung up on me.

Yep, I sure did sound crazy. I was crazy out of my mind panicked and believing that within the next few days I was going to be homeless and my rescues were all going to be dead and I couldn't do a damn thing to stop what was happening. No money, no lawyer, no help.

Just unbelievable corruption and *evil*.

~ ~ ~

Shortly after my frantic phone calls, I got a message that my husband said I was supposed to move into our little investment property that we had been trying to sell. Yes, it was better than being homeless, but it had been gutted down to the studs and was like a brand-new house. It was carpeted and furnished with beautiful new furniture. It was less than nine hundred square feet, and there was no way I could care for dozens of rescues in that little house.

I was going to lose one of the last opportunities I had to make any money from all of the renovation work I'd done, because I knew the little house was going to be ruined. It was not "pet-friendly" when your pets number in the dozens.

~ ~ ~

It was the day before the bank said they were going to foreclose. I had been working day and night to try to pack and move things to the little house that we were supposed to be selling. I had an overwhelming sense of dread that the little house I had worked so hard on was going to be ruined in short order, and that it was never going to be adequate for me to take care of all our rescues. I also had no idea how I was going to pay for anything, like utilities or a mortgage payment or food, and just kept trying to force myself to go through the motions. I just couldn't sit down and sob about it anymore. I had run out of time and had no options.

My husband was still drinking, still chasing women, still giving in to his addictions, still lying. But he was apparently also getting really tired and frustrated that things weren't working out like he'd planned. He hadn't been able to find a nice young female body for sex, and the drinking and late nights were really starting to catch up with the out-of-shape, overweight lawyer who already hated just about every other part of his life.

So he called me. He asked me how I was doing. *Really?* Would I like to meet him at Pizza Hut and he'd buy me dinner? Okay.

I stopped at Cercone's office and reported that my husband wanted to take me to dinner, and that I was hoping I wasn't going to be arrested for meeting him. I was told I'd better "be careful" that I didn't step out of line. Okay.

I sat across the table from the man who had abused me for years, who was responsible for inflicting so much pain on my innocent animals and on me, who kept me in a cell for six horrific weeks, who had totally destroyed my beautiful home, and I did my damnedest to smile and stay calm and carry on a civil conversation. I said I was fine, but that I was very worried about how I was going to finish moving—and get the cats moved—and how I was going to take care of things financially. I told him the "little house" needed things, like a kitchen faucet, and that I was just going to keep trying to do the best I could.

That was when my husband told me he *wanted* to help me. He would get a friend to help, and they would get the rest of my things moved. He would take care of whatever else we needed.

I managed to get through the next few days feeling numb. I just couldn't blow up, I couldn't say anything that would cause him to snap, and I had to do whatever it took to survive. I knew who he was, and I knew what he was capable of doing to us.

We went shopping. My indigent husband who could afford to give me only $175 a week to care for myself and our rescues took me shopping for jeans and shirts and sweaters that fit me, bought me a new kitchen faucet and helped me install it, bought me a clearance-priced sofa to replace the new furniture he'd given to my daughter while I was in jail, and opened a checking account in my name with $300. The customer service woman at the bank (we'd known her for a long time) commented that my husband was "such a good man" while I sat there trying not to scream, and I just looked at him and smiled, and he said, "No, I'm really not." And she just went on to say, "Oh yes, you are *really* a good man!"

Whatever. As long as my rescues and I were going to survive another day, I could do this another day.

~ ~ ~

Shortly after that I realized that I could do just about anything I needed to do to survive. I already had, hadn't I? I had dozens of innocent animals that totally depended on me alone, and there was no way I wasn't going to do *anything* I could to be able to take care of them.

So I became a real prostitute wife, a whore that would provide him with sex in exchange for food and cleaning supplies and cat litter. I knew what my husband wanted more than anything else. Okay, so he didn't want his wife in her fifties, but he would definitely settle for his wife in her fifties if he couldn't find the woman of his dreams in her thirties or forties. (Or teens or twenties.)

I knew how we could get the bills paid and how I could get my car back and how I could continue to care for my animals. And I did whatever I needed to do. My husband decided he had been such a fool, and he was "so sorry," and he loved me more than ever, and he felt like we were like newlyweds, and he just couldn't believe he had been so blind. Yeah, right.

~ ~ ~

My husband went to his best friend and attorney, Greg, and told him that we were reconciling. Greg gave my husband what turned out to be a prophetic piece of advice. He told him that reconciling with me would be "career suicide."

Translated: The powers that be were only going to keep acting as though they liked him and employing him as long as he kept his distance from me and they could maintain their phony little narrative about how he was wronged, and had no addictions, and was no liability to the county.

Fortunately, or unfortunately, my husband wanted sex more than he wanted to keep toeing the line for the county.

Four days after they found out we had "reconciled," he was fired from his position as chief public defender for the county. Sheriff Brad Mason literally escorted him from the building with his possessions in a cardboard box.

The only thing that was different about his situation was that he had reconciled with me.

Back in the Office

MY DAUGHTER WAS off from work to have her baby around the same time we reconciled. I had only seen her one time during the prior six months when I stopped by the office very briefly after I got out of jail. I had seen her car in front of the office and knew my husband would be gone because of his schedule, so I just walked in and gave her a hug, telling her I loved her. She was unusually cold and told me I had better leave because he would be back anytime and she didn't want any trouble. I can't explain what I felt, but she wasn't looking at me like I was her mother. She was looking at me like I was a potential problem for her.

When my husband and I decided that I would start doing some legal work for him again, the reaction from my daughter and our other female employee was stunning.

The "other" Kelly. I had tried to help a young girl in her twenties the year before. She had lost her part-time job across the street from our office. I thought we got along really well.

She had done work for me on the house renovations I had undertaken for our investor, and also did filing and basic office work when we needed her. I had overpaid her, often trying to help her out. I would tell her that even if I didn't have enough work for her to justify paying her a certain number of hours, I would still pay her the same amount so she didn't have to go without. She would regularly bring her young son to the house job, and he would get into things that he shouldn't with little or no discipline by his mother. I bit my tongue a hundred times, telling myself that she was young and I respected her for wanting to work and provide for him, so I almost never said anything.

I quickly learned that both girls really loved having me gone from the office because it allowed them to basically run everything on their own terms. When I ran the office, I would often let my daughter know that I wasn't pleased when she would regularly come in late and spend a lot of time online with e-mail, shopping, and playing games. I knew she was taking advantage of me, and most of the time I didn't say much. But sometimes we would really argue over her spending too much down time while at work. For the six months I was gone, they had been able to goof off just about whenever they felt like it, and pretty much had no one to answer to. My husband was drinking nearly every day, desperately trying to bed younger women, enjoying his P and M and living like a bachelor. He was not going to spend much time overseeing them when he was so engrossed in his new lifestyle.

When my daughter found out I was going to be back in the office, at least part-time, she really flipped out. It was worse than getting punched in the stomach or slapped in the face. I loved my daughter and was so proud of her, and although she had been through many rebellious times over her teenage years, she had really settled down and treated me well. I believed we loved each other, had respect for each other, and got along really well.

When she went into labor and I learned she was in the hospital, I went with my husband–her stepfather–to see her. She was in a private room and hadn't given birth yet, and when I walked into the room, I gave her a hug, told her I loved her, and asked if it was okay that I had come to see her, she only said, "As long as you don't cause trouble." I guess she really hated me. It was indescribably painful, but I felt as though I must have deserved it. I didn't stay more than five minutes, and she wasn't going to ask me to stay, or to come back, or anything. I have never heard from her since that day. More than seven years ago.

My daughter took files from the office and just about stripped clean the hard drive from her computer. She said she would never come back to work for my husband as long as "that cow" was still there. "That cow" was me. When we tried to figure out whose work she had done and whose bankruptcies needed to be filed, we couldn't find the files, and often couldn't find work that we thought she had done.

My husband had to call the city police to get the files back from her that she had taken. I can't describe what it feels like to lose your child when your child is still alive. It is something I have tried desperately to live with for years now. I have to ask God for help to not think about my own children and grandchildren because it is still just too painful. I always loved the idea of family, and it's why I left home at seventeen. I wanted a family that wasn't dysfunctional, like my own. I wanted to be the perfect wife and mother. How I wish I'd have believed in asking God to help me make those life-altering choices, like whom to marry and when to have children!

I guess I *always* thought I knew better, and I *never* did.

Trying to Get Help Again

MONTHS AFTER OUR "reconciliation," I spent more than a week writing out a twenty-one-page narrative that summarized what had been done to me and my animals. Every time I would try to work on it, I would get so physically ill that I'd have to leave my computer and my desk for hours at a time. I was determined to find a law firm that would represent me in lawsuits against the judges, lawyers, and other people who had stripped me of my rights. Since I knew that everything I was saying could be documented—especially court proceedings and correspondence—I naively believed that I would have big firms begging me to let them represent me.

I went to a local copy store and had more than two dozen copies of my narrative put together, including attachments of the documents Dom Cercone had falsified and lots of other supporting documentation. I mailed copies to large law firms in the Harrisburg, Philadelphia, and Pittsburgh areas, to the ACLU, to (former) Governor Rendell's office, to the Disciplinary Board of PA and the PA Judicial Conduct Board, to Pennsylvania law schools, and to our state and federal representatives and senators.

After giving me the runaround because I'd initially contacted the "wrong" office, the ACLU directed me to their Pittsburgh office, where they told me that they couldn't help me because my problem wasn't the kind that would help many other people if they intervened on my behalf. They told me they only liked to get involved in matters that had wide-reaching impact. My case wasn't like that, they said.

Many large law firms and civil rights attorneys wrote back to me and expressed basically the same opinion: My claims may well have merit, but getting over the hurdle of judicial immunity might be insurmountable. They could not justify significant time and cost advances when several of the defendants would be judges.

I became more and more distressed and heartsick as I continued to look up every civil rights attorney I could find just about anywhere, even in New York State. I kept getting the same response. I wanted to sue judges for harming me, and the judges were going to be able to get away with just about anything and would never be held accountable. I wrote to the FBI, the Department of Justice, and our state legislature. I begged them to please have *someone* investigate what had happened, and I never even got a response.

At that time, Arlen Specter was our congressman, and he had a "local" office in Erie. I had written his office many times and had faxed him tons of supporting documentation when one of the secretaries told me she thought Specter would help me. I never heard from him. Arlen Specter had recently switched parties to run in the primary and was defeated, and now was serving out the balance of his last term.

One afternoon when I had made a trip with my husband to Erie to cover bankruptcy hearings for his clients, I happened to notice that Specter's office door was open, which was unusual. The office was usually closed when we were there. I walked to the open door where two young female employees were sitting at desks, not doing much of anything. I poked my head in the door and said, "Would you please give Mr. Specter a message for me?" and one of them said, "Sure." I said something like "Too bad Mr. Specter couldn't find enough voters to support him. I guess he was giving them the same thing he was giving me." I held up my middle finger and said, "This is all Mr. Specter ever gave me."

One girl started yelling at me and said they weren't going to "tolerate" that kind of "language" in their office and ran down the hall to get one of the federal marshals working security. I went back to my seat in the hall, and I guess they must have decided they couldn't arrest me for expressing my opinion, because they never came to get me.

I faxed my narrative to Representative Glenn Thompson's offices. *Offices*, plural. I faxed it to his three different offices, begged his staff for a response, and never heard one word from Glenn Thompson.

~ ~ ~

I also tried to contact more than a dozen animal rescue organizations across the country. I sent letters to foundations established by Doris Day and Bob Barker and every celebrity-endorsed organization I could find online. I wrote to Ellen DeGeneres and Mary Tyler Moore and others well known for rescuing homeless and abandoned animals or for supporting rescue organizations. I hoped that they would somehow help me get some publicity, since I had absolutely no way to let anyone in my own community know because of John Satterwhite and his monopoly on the newspapers and radio station.

I heard back from just one national organization, and they could only tell me how sorry they were that my animals and I had gone through such abuse, but that their "mission" wasn't to get involved in cases of abuse but, rather, to raise money to fund their own projects. That was not only extremely disappointing to me, but also extremely distressing. I had watched the ASPCA ads on TV for years showing abused animals, and it still breaks my heart to this day to watch even a few seconds of one of those commercials. I had always done what they were purporting to advocate—save homeless, abandoned, and abused animals from harm, and no organization was going to help me when their main "mission" was to raise money to fund themselves.

I firmly believe there was no way anyone else was going to get involved because our abusers were judges and lawyers and law enforcement officials.

There was just no way.

Cheryl Magnotta

MANY PEOPLE WON'T care about what I write about Cheryl. I believe that most people think she was an animal abuser who left her Great Danes to starve to death and would have absolutely no sympathy for her no matter what happened to her. If I had ever been convinced that she was guilty of the crimes with which she'd been charged, I would have had to believe she was literally out of her mind, and legally insane. I loved innocent animals way too much to have been able to befriend Cheryl and become so close to her if she had been an animal abuser herself.

When I left the jail on December 12, 2007, I was heartsick to leave Cheryl behind. We had truly become friends, and I loved her. She had always denied to me that she was guilty of abusing any animals, ever. I had learned so much about her life over the course of more than a month, and more than anyone in the world, Cheryl had helped me survive my incarceration. She cried with me, and she yelled at me when she thought I would get in trouble if I broke down. She constantly reminded me that I could get written up if I became hysterical. Although my husband was her attorney, he did almost nothing to help her. He had told me he thought she was crazy, and I could make all kinds of snide remarks about the pot calling the kettle black, but I think it goes without saying. I had watched Cheryl spend hours writing letters to my husband begging him to help her, begging him to get her into court. He never responded to her in all the time I was with her, and she did not get into court while I was there either. The worst thing she ever said about my husband was that he was a weasel. That was always her name for him. Weasel.

I had also watched Cheryl's physical health deteriorate while I was with her, and by the time I left, she appeared to be very sick. Cheryl wrote me several long letters after I went home, trying to keep me informed about what was going on with her. Her biggest concern and fear was for her mother, who was in her eighties. Her mother was in Scranton, more than six hours away, and she and Cheryl had hired a contractor to renovate a property they'd purchased to make it comfortable for the two of them to live together. Her mother had to make all the decisions on the house while worrying constantly about her daughter. She never understood just why Cheryl was in jail. They would talk on the phone a couple times a week, and her mother would just sob and beg her to come home, and Cheryl would sob after she got off the phone.

Near the end of December, Cheryl became deathly sick in jail, after I'd gone home. She was taken to the Bradford Regional Medical Center, a half hour away, in an ambulance. After she was admitted, I got a call from one of the corrections officers who was with her at the hospital. Because Cheryl was an inmate, she had to have a CO with her at all times. I talked with Cheryl for a few minutes and could tell she was in very bad shape.

Cheryl underwent tests at BRMC and it was discovered she was going into renal failure. I knew she was a diabetic, and I knew that this was really serious. She was told at the hospital that she needed extensive treatment. Extensive treatment that was *expensive* treatment.

McKean County was contacted, but my husband, her lawyer, was not. The McKean County Commissioners agreed that McKean County was not going to foot the bill for Cheryl's extensive, expensive treatment.

Cheryl still had not had her day in court, but even if she was on her deathbed, she was going to get it now. In the middle of a blizzard, Cheryl showed up at my front door. Her mother was in their van in my driveway. Cheryl looked so small and frail and very, very pale. She gave me a hug and told me, very quickly, what had happened.

When the county was advised that Cheryl was very sick and needed expensive medical treatment, "the powers that be" scrambled and arranged for her to go directly from the hospital to the courtroom. The judge told her they were going to take her plea, and they were going to let her go home, to Scranton, many hours away, in a blizzard. Six hours in good weather, at least ten hours in bad. They wanted her to get her medical treatment at home. There was no way in hell McKean County was going to pay for it.

By this time, Cheryl had served more than 180 days in jail without going to court, a clear violation of Pennsylvania law. But this was a woman that no one in McKean County cared about, so it was no big deal to anyone.

Cheryl's mother had driven their van to Bradford in the blizzard, and Cheryl drove her mother back home to Scranton in the blizzard, barely able to see over the steering wheel. She was deathly sick, and after she got home, her health continued to worsen. Cheryl called me several times from home during the next several months, and every time I talked to her, she was a little bit worse. She kept telling me that she had gone to several doctors and specialists, and they all told her the same thing. She had waited too long to get treatment, and now it was extremely difficult to treat. She would go for some kind of treatment that she'd told me was coming up, and a week later, she would tell me that the doctors told her it wasn't working.

Cheryl stopped calling. One morning my husband and I were having breakfast, and I was reading the *Era*. I turned to page 2, the obituaries, and there was Cheryl's name. She was only fifty-nine. She had died in Scranton.

I can't describe the grief that overwhelmed me, and I can't begin to describe the anger I felt toward my husband, and toward the county. I showed him the obituary. He just looked, shrugged, said, "Oh, that's too bad," and went back to eating his breakfast. I sobbed, and my heart broke for her. I would later find out that she and her long-ago and faraway boyfriend from her younger years had reconciled right before she died, and I guess that was the only thing that seemed like a blessing at the end of Cheryl's life.

Anyone reading this might think that it doesn't matter one way or another if Cheryl died, or even if the McKean County Jail had anything to do with her death. You don't have to care about Cheryl, or that she died, but what you *should* care about is that something like this could happen to *anyone* in the McKean County Jail, or to anyone that ever has to deal with the McKean County court system.

You also don't have to care about what happened to me or to my rescue animals, but you should absolutely care that it could happen to *your* sister, or *your* daughter, or *your* mother, or *your* best friend, or to *you*. You can kid yourself and say that you would never do anything to cause you to end up in that jail, but hitting my husband in the face in the midst of a mutually combative domestic violence situation should not have put *me* in that jail either.

As long as the same people hold the same offices in McKean County, like Chris Hauser and John Pavlock and Dom Cercone, you absolutely *should* care. And as of the date of the publication of this book, every one of them still holds public office.

~ ~ ~

I am attaching a copy of an e-mail that was sent to the new county solicitor, Dan Hartle, which I inadvertently received in a large batch of documents I'd requested, either through FOIA or my request for production. I say "inadvertently," but I believe I received it because it was supposed to be seen. Seen by more people than just me.

Extremely coincidentally, it was sent to Dan Hartle just a short time after Cheryl was refused treatment for her acute illness and sent home to Scranton in a blizzard. The subject of the inquiry was clearly about another inmate that needed medical care while incarcerated in the McKean County Jail, and the consensus seemed to be that no preexisting medical conditions were going to be paid for by the county.

This makes it much clearer, at least to me, why Cheryl got almost no treatment, and why she eventually died from kidney failure a short time later.

McKean County was never going to pay for her care.

E-mail

From:
Date: Fri Jan 18, 08 - 1:03 PM - E-mail
To: 'Daniel J. Hartle'
CC:
Subject: McKean County Prison Inmate ████████████ Medical Treatment

Contact: Daniel J. Hartle
File: ████████████ Burg RSP, Asslt - 3 Cases ████████████

ATTENTION: The information contained in this e-mail transmittal is
privileged and confidential, and intended only for the use of the
individual(s) and/or entities named as the intended recipient(s). If
you are not the intended recipient(s), you are hereby notified that any
unauthorized disclosure, copying, distribution or taking of any action
based on, or in reliance on, the information contained in this e-mail
transmittal is strictly prohibited. Any review of the information
contained in this e-mail transmittal, other than by the intended
recipient(s), SHALL NOT constitute a waiver of the attorney-client
privilege or any other applicable privileges. If you received this
e-mail transmission in error, please notify me immediately, by telephone
at ████████████ or by e-mail sent to ████████████.
Also, please remove, and permanently delete, all copies of this e-mail
transmittal, if received in error, from any computer, e-mail server, or
any other location. I will reimburse you for any reasonable actual
expenses incurred in doing so. Thank you.

Dan: I represent ████████████ who is currently incarcerated in the
McKean County Prison. I attach a copy of a letter sent to Dr.
Castellano, which basically outlines the issues. In summary, I
understand that a diagnostic test has been requested by Dr. Khoja, on or
about December 14, 2007, my client's neurosurgeon, which has yet to be
performed. After speaking with Warden Woodruff on January 16, and,
representatives of Cost Management Plus (who I understand is McKean
County's Program Administrator for payments for inmate medical
treatment), yesterday and today, I have a question about the county's
apparent policy not to pay for an inmate's pre-existing medical
conditions. Warden Woodruff indicated that that was the policy and that
McKean County does not pay for treatment of pre-existing conditions. He
referred me to a Carol Rusnak of Cost Management Plus. I asked her for
authority for that position yesterday, and another representative of
that company told me, when I telephoned again today, that Ms. Rusnak had
passed along my questions to their solicitor. The solicitor is
apparently a member of the Harrisburg law firm of Metter Evans and
Woodside. The solicitor's response was to contact the county solicitor.
Therefore, I am contacting you, as I understand you are the new McKean
County solicitor.

In regard to McKean County refusing to pay for pre-existing medical
conditions, my research to date has not yielded any authority for that
position. If there is authority, whether statutory, regulatory or case
law, please inform me at once. Otherwise, please inform me of ████ other
basis that would support the delay in the completion of the ████████
testing, and the reasons why the testing has not been ████ormed. Thank
you.

I note that as I di████ ████ave Warden Woodruff's e-mail address, that I

Sentencing

December 2009

I WAS TERRIFIED. Not for myself, but for my animals. I had already been in jail. I knew I could, and would, survive it as long as I knew my animals were being cared for. But I was so afraid that my husband would again neglect them, not care for them properly, not feed them enough, not clean up after them.

I had pled guilty to one count of theft for taking money from my husband's account. An attorney that did a lot of work for the Public Defender's Office, Dennis Luttenauer, had agreed to represent me privately, and treated me with great kindness and respect. I was so thankful that I was being treated so well because I had come to believe that no one was ever going to treat me well again, at least not in McKean County.

The week before my sentencing was scheduled, I wrote to Judge Alexander, the senior judge from outside the county who had been appointed to oversee my case. I told him I knew I had broken the law, that I had to be punished, and that I wasn't going to try to make any excuses to him for my behavior or actions. But I begged him to please give me work release with an extra hour on either end—an extra hour in the morning and an extra hour at the end of the day—so I could stop by at home and make sure the animals were being taken care of. I told Judge Alexander what had happened to my animals when I had been jailed in 2007, how my home had been destroyed, and how they'd been left in squalor.

I knew I wouldn't get special treatment. If anything, I expected something really bad. The day before sentencing, I went to the store and bought packages of white T-shirts and underwear and socks and took them with me to the courthouse. I knew I could expect to be sent directly from the courthouse to the jail. I'd seen it done so many times before when I'd sat through criminal court days with my husband, and I'd seen it when I was in jail two years before.

Judge Alexander went through all the standard sentencing explanations and procedures. He then made a lengthy statement. More like a speech, I guess. He wanted to make sure that the prosecution (Attorney General Corbett's office) and probation had received a copy of my letter. He said he was very disturbed by what had happened in 2007, and said, "None of that *ever* should have happened." He then went on to explain the sentence he was imposing on me.

Seven years' probation. No restrictions. I just had to pay restitution within seven years.

He said he knew he could sentence me to jail time, but he felt that the time I had already served was enough. He again said it shouldn't have happened, and made some comments to let everyone in the courtroom know that he wasn't happy about what he had learned.

I'm pretty sure my heart stopped for a long few seconds. I was just absolutely *not* sure I had heard what he'd said. Did he say I was being sentenced to *probation*? Did he say *no restrictions*?

Oh my God! My God, did he say I *wasn't* going to jail? I just buried my face in my hands and sobbed. I could barely catch my breath. I kept saying, "Thank you, thank you, thank you" to the judge, to God, to no one in particular.

The judge kept talking for a few minutes, and I know most of it was procedural, but I did hear him say that anyone who wanted an explanation for his sentence could refer to the transcript, which he would make available.

I looked across the aisle at my husband, and he looked stunned, not happy. I looked at the attorney general's representative, Todd Goodwin, and he looked stunned, not happy. I looked at my own lawyer—for the first time in a long time, I actually had someone advocating for me—and he looked pleased.

The judge dismissed us, and we went out into the hallway. I threw my arms around my husband, looking for some relief or something positive from him, and there wasn't much. I heard him say, "You don't know what a miracle you just got." I told him I knew it was a miracle, and that I just wanted to go home. I was so thankful to be going home, to be able to give my animals their dinner and clean up after them and lie down. My head was pounding so hard, and I was so drained, and I was so thankful. Judge Alexander was an angel that day. A real God-sent angel.

~ ~ ~

A few days later, my husband would let me know how happy he was that I didn't go to jail. Sitting on the couch at home, he sneered at me and said, "You should have gone to jail! You should have gone to jail!" And he stormed out, leaving me sobbing. Again.

Until that moment, I hadn't fully realized what he most likely had planned, believing I would be away for weeks, or even months. He had planned to go back to his bachelor lifestyle, and here I was, ruining it for him again. He always hated me for interfering with his "plans."

~ ~ ~

December 9, 2009

I was really getting panicked at the thought that my two-year statute of limitations was going to run out on the twelfth of December for me to be able to file any actions against anyone who had harmed me and my animals. I had tried everything I could think of to get my husband to help me with a lawsuit against the county, and as the clock was ticking, he seemed to get more interested in what might be in it for him. He despised them for firing him and humiliating him by having the sheriff escort him from the building, and he wanted some kind of revenge. I was able to get him to dictate sections of the complaint for several hours at a time, sometimes several times a day, before he would start to lose control. We worked on it for weeks, and he pronounced it "done" after dozens of revisions and hours of proofing. I had to go to the federal court's website before filing it to make sure that we were going to follow every procedure and rule to the letter so we wouldn't get tossed out before we even started. Everything had to be filed electronically, but hundreds of hours of filing bankruptcy paperwork for clients the same way had prepared me.

After the suit against the county was ready to be filed, I asked him to help me draft a similar complaint against numerous defendants, most of them his friends and/or colleagues. He told me he would not, and said I would be "making a huge mistake" if I filed anything against them. He said I couldn't prove that they had done the things I was alleging, and that federal law made it too tough to prove.

It was December 9, and I had three days left to draft, proof, and finish a complaint naming multiple defendants. I figured I could use the format we'd used for the suit against the county and somehow I could make it work. I knew it was going to be really tough without my husband helping me at all, but I just couldn't let these people get away with what they had done to me. I just could not imagine them walking away scot-free. I especially had to let the public know what kind of people were in positions of authority in our county, most of them elected.

I had to decide, in very short order, whether or not I was going to follow through. All of a sudden an idea popped into my head, and I thought it sounded sensible, so I went with it.

I decided I would go to Dom Cercone and ask to speak with him privately. I had known him for decades before everything had happened, and I was hoping against hope that by now, two years later, he would have had plenty of time to think about what he had done to us, and would have felt bad, or guilty, or remorseful. I pictured him sitting across the desk from me, telling me he had no idea that my animals would be harmed, and that he was truly sorry. I called his office and asked his secretary for an appointment to meet with him. She told me he would be back in the office at 1:00 p.m. and told me I didn't need an appointment, and that I could just stop in.

I got in the car, said a prayer out loud and asked God to help me. I told myself if Dom apologized to me, and really seemed remorseful or regretful, that I would not pursue a lawsuit against him personally. I was sure I would know, by looking him in the eye, if he was really sorry.

~ ~ ~

I walked in the door a little after 1:00 p.m. and went up to the window where his secretary was. I reminded her that I had called, and that she said I could talk to Dom. He came to the window and asked me what I wanted. I told him I wanted to talk with him privately. He simply said "No.." He said whatever I wanted to talk to him about, I could say at the window. There were other people in the waiting room, and his staff was all within earshot. I asked him again if we could talk privately, and he finally said that he would give me a minute with his secretary present and the door open. I agreed and followed them into a small room with a desk and a couple of chairs.

He sat down behind the desk and asked me what I wanted to talk about. I said, "I need to talk to you about what happened." He said he didn't know what I was talking about. I told him I wanted to talk to him about what had happened when he put me in jail with no hearing and no bail. I said, "You know, many of my animals died like I told you they would." He said, "I didn't do anything to you!" and he started to get up to leave the room. I had never even raised my voice, and he was going to bully me right out of there.

To say that I was shocked would be such an understatement. I felt as though I had been smacked in the face and punched in the stomach at the same time. And then I realized what I was seeing, again. Arrogance, self-righteousness, entitlement, abuse. I started trembling, and started to cry. He yelled at me to get out, and when I said again, "I just wanted to talk to you about what you did to me because I *had* to know if you were sorry," he started yelling as he was leading me out to the waiting room, very loudly, so everyone present could hear: "I think Cathy's having another episode! I think we'd better call Stoney! I think she may need to be committed!"

I guess I wasn't moving fast enough, because he said if I didn't get out right then, he would call the police, and the last thing he yelled was, "You want to go back to jail?"

I staggered to my car, in absolute shock, and drove myself back to the office. I was hysterical by then, wailing and sobbing. I ran into the office and back to my husband's desk, where he was sitting, as usual, playing a video game. I started to tell him what had just happened, and the first thing he screamed at me was, "What the hell were you thinking!"

I tried to tell him that I had decided that I wouldn't file a suit against Dom if I was convinced that he was sorry for what he had done to me, and that I had called ahead and asked to speak with him. Instead of getting any kind of comfort or support from my husband, I got what I always got. Accusations, criticism, and verbal attacks. We had been married twenty-one years by then, and I had never once seen my husband either stand up for me or defend me. *Never.* And he sure wasn't going to start now. I was interrupting his computer game.

Within the next two hours, while I was still shaking and sick to my stomach, we got several phone calls, all inspired by Cercone. As soon as I had left his office, he had called the Probation Department, the police, and the Attorney General's Office to report me. I had done nothing wrong. I had not broken any laws. I had called ahead. I had tried to speak to him quietly. And he tried to have me arrested *again*.

I was screaming and sobbing. I was absolutely terror-stricken that I was going to be sent back to the jail, and I knew for sure this time I wouldn't make it out alive. My heart was racing, and my head felt as though it was going to explode. It wouldn't make any difference that I hadn't broken a law. I would never be given any rights in McKean County, and I would never be protected by any "equal protection" or "due process." It didn't exist there. Not for me, not ever.

When my husband got off the phone with the various law enforcement people, he screamed and yelled and lectured me, telling me how "lucky" I was that he had been able to convince them not to charge me with anything. He told me he hoped I'd learned my lesson.

I despised them all. I probably even prayed that God would kill them all.

I spent the next two days feverishly doing my best to put together a second federal lawsuit. The first one that my husband helped me put together was me versus the county, the Board of County Commissioners, who were supposed to be responsible for overseeing the jail, and the jail warden at the time of my incarceration. The second suit was me versus Judge

Dom Cercone, attorney Chris Hauser, who had conspired with Dom to keep me imprisoned, John Egbert, the chairman of the Board of County Commissioners and Debbie Babcox, the family law master who had refused to take my evidence at a spousal support hearing and had awarded me zero.

I filed the complaint against the county in the afternoon while my husband was in the office. He watched me put it together, get it scanned and electronically filed, pay the $350 filing fee, and confirm that it was on. I told him to go home and I would be there shortly. He didn't know that I had finished putting together a second suit, and I waited until he was long gone before I electronically filed it myself.

He wouldn't find out until the next day when I told him at home, knowing he would fly into a rage when he found out. And he did.

My husband flying into a rage had become part of my life again, and I had learned to pray every single day that I would survive it long enough to find a way out, and then to get out. I was now praying that the lawsuits were going to provide me with the means for my way out of hell.

Reconciliation...Not So Much

My husband had quite a bit of work to do in the office and could not do any of it by himself. Actually, he couldn't do his own share of the work and was counting on me more and more to carry the workload. His mental, emotional, and physical health had deteriorated substantially, and I knew he was back to his porn. The only place he could look at it was in the office, because I would no longer have a computer at home, so at one point I actually got desperate enough to try to convince myself that a porn block or filter would stop it. It didn't. I think I paid $60, and he found a way around it.

He was spending more and more time in front of the computer playing games when he couldn't look at porn, and if we had an argument in the office, he would often become so much more than enraged. He had been given a preliminary diagnosis of bipolar disorder in 2008, and it had really progressed to something very scary. His countenance would become almost contorted, his face would turn purple, and his stance—the way he was standing—would become bizarre. He would spit and sputter and be almost growling, while spewing four-letter words at me and threatening to kill me. Sometimes he would throw things at me, and sometimes he would literally press his body up against me and ram me into the wall or doorjamb. I knew it wasn't just the BPD. It was also his massive addictions that he wasn't able to feed. Very, very much like a drug addict going through withdrawal.

Do not *ever* believe it when someone tells you, "Oh, just chill, everyone does it!" Being addicted to pornography is not a joke. It can lead to the most horrific things, and can even be deadly.

Many times he would just storm out of the office when he had clients scheduled to come in and laugh at me on the way out, telling me to "have fun explaining to them" why he wasn't there. One afternoon he screamed at me to get out or he would call the police. When I asked him why he was going to call the police, and what he was going to tell them, he said, "I don't know, I'll make something up." When he did things like that, I would go to the township police chief, Jeff Wolbert, and ask him to make some kind of record or write it down somewhere. I was deathly afraid that he was going to do something again to have me locked up, and no one could ever convince me anymore that he wasn't capable of doing something horrible again. He had already done so many horrible things to me that I always believed it was just a matter of time.

Sometimes at home he would refuse to get up in the morning to go to the office even when he had clients scheduled, and would tell me the same thing. "Have fun explaining why I'm not there! You can tell them it's all your fault!" One day he picked up the TV remote control and spiked it at me, leaving a huge black-and-blue welt the size of a baseball on the side of my leg. I again made sure I went to the local police chief and showed him the bruise, asking him to make a record. The chief knew I had no intention of filing any charges against my husband because it would be far more dangerous for me to do that than to do nothing. Going to the police chief was my half-hearted attempt at somehow covering myself if he had me put in jail again. When I was there in 2007, I was covered with huge bruises and yet apparently no one believed that we had been involved in "mutual domestic violence." It was always characterized as *me* beating *him*.

The Lawsuits

I WOULD LIKE to be able to give you a detailed account of what it was like to file lawsuits in a federal court with no attorney, and then agonize every single day trying to keep going, to not give up, to not give in to the abusers and liars and criminals. Because I still have horrific flashbacks and nightmares about certain things that happened to me during the course of the civil litigation, I won't go into every detail. Anyone who is interested can look at the pleadings through the federal court's website in the Western District of Pennsylvania, Erie Division, *Catherine F. Langella vs. The County of McKean*, et al., at No. 1:09-cv-00311E, Judge Maurice Cohill presiding.

There are so many procedures and rules that must be followed in federal court, and you can so easily be thrown to the curb if you don't strictly follow all of them to the letter. It was not only expensive, it was staggeringly time-consuming and horrifically stressful.

The county had immediately turned the case over to their high-priced law firm in Erie and would be represented by attorney Pat Carey, an arrogant, haughty and condescending young guy who honestly seemed to take great delight in watching me in pain. I learned to expect his snide remarks, attacks, and smirks, and never got used to them. I would often think to myself, *If Pat Carey acts like this in his office or in court, how in the hell does he act at home?*

Lawyers *all* have public personas that are an improvement over their private personas, and I could only imagine how abusive and obnoxious he must be with his own wife and family, behind closed doors.

During one meeting with Pat Carey at his office in Erie, I was shaking and crying and described what I had gone through as "torture". He started laughing, and with a huge smirk on his face, said "Mrs. Langella, you were NOT tortured! At least not according to the *legal* definition!"

This is the legal definition of *torture*:

> Torture means any act by which severe pain or suffering, whether physical or mental, is intentionally inflicted on a person for such purposes as obtaining from him or a third person information or a confession, punishing him for an act he or a third person has committed or is suspected of having committed, or intimidating or coercing him or a third person, or for any reason based on discrimination of any kind, when such pain or suffering is inflicted

by or at the instigation of or with the consent or acquiescence of a public official or other person acting in an official capacity. It does not include pain or suffering arising only from, inherent in or incidental to lawful sanctions.

~ ~ ~

John Egbert and Debbie Babcox were also represented by Pat Carey because they were both employees of the county, so they all got top-notch representation for free. Well, if "free" means "paid for by the taxpayers."

Dominic Cercone was represented "for free" by Mary Butler of the Administrative Office of the Pennsylvania Courts (AOPC) because he was a district magistrate. Mary Butler turned out to be the female equivalent of Pat Carey. Lucky me. I never met her in person, but she was also haughty, arrogant, and paid for by the taxpayers. She never returned one phone call from me and never responded to one letter from me over the course of more than a year. I didn't matter to her, and she was going to get her hefty taxpayer-paid-for salary regardless of how she treated me. I guess that's part of the "war on women" the politicians often talk about.

Neither Egbert or Babcox or Cercone or Woodruff were going to care how much it would cost to litigate the suits because none of them had to pay a cent. They knew I had no lawyer, and they knew the costs would be a hardship on me. They also knew that, one way or another, as long as it took, they were going to win.

Although I knew that Cercone and Hauser had colluded—collusion: secret or illegal cooperation or conspiracy, especially in order to cheat or deceive others— and that collusion was against the law, the court said I couldn't prove they had colluded, and threw out those aspects of the suit.

Cercone also had immunity as a judge. Judge Cohill actually wrote in his Opinion and Order that a judge can literally use *malice* when depriving you of your rights, and judicial immunity still applies. In other words, Dom Cercone had figuratively raped me, and it was okay under the law.

Judicial immunity.

Chris Hauser's high-priced lawyer from Erie had written me a lengthy, very threatening letter telling me just exactly what I was going to do, including dropping the action against Chris, and warned me that I was in big trouble for involving Chris. I told him, sort of, to bleep himself. There was nothing he could say to me that was going to scare me more than I had already been.

Although I knew that Debbie Babcox had abused her discretion and abused her power as a family law master, the law said she also had immunity as a member of the judiciary.

I could not prove that John Egbert had gone to the *Bradford Era* to threaten them with a lawsuit because no one was going to testify for me to support that allegation.

Marcie Schellhammer had *told* me that it happened, but there was no way she was going to be honest and testify to that when it came to saving herself and her job. And even if I could prove that John Egbert had done what I had alleged, it really wasn't a crime.

My suit against the county and the commissioners and the warden would still proceed, but I knew that it was going to be months, or years, of more agony and stress and lost time and flashbacks. I would pray constantly, asking God to give me the strength to keep going, to "fight the good fight," and then I would very often collapse at home and just sob for hours. I felt so horribly alone and worn out, and I just could not understand how these horrible people were still "winning."

One of the worst days of the entire process was when I was finally able to schedule taking the depositions of Debbie Morlock, my former friend, who had also been the former deputy warden, as well as the former warden, Tim Woodruff.

~ ~ ~

Debbie Morlock

Shortly after I filed the actions in federal court, I ran into Debbie one afternoon when I was in Walmart. I was so happy to see a "friendly" face and gave her a big hug. We were in the vacuum cleaner aisle in the back of the store, it was in the middle of the afternoon, and there was almost no one else around.

She asked me how I was doing, and I told her I was doing okay, but that Ron wasn't. I told her it was tough, but I was "doing what I have to do until I don't have to do it anymore." She said she understood, smiled and nodded. I had heard that she had been fired or let go from the jail, and I asked her if *she* was okay. She said she was, but that she wanted to ask me a few questions if I had a minute.

Before she asked, I told her there was something I wanted to tell her. I told her that I had finally filed a lawsuit against the county, and that I had also filed a suit against Dom Cercone, John Egbert, Chris Hauser, and Debbie Babcox. I told her I was so hopeful that something was going to come from it, and that the people who had harmed me were going to be held accountable.

Debbie then said, "I need to ask you a question about when you were in the jail."

"Okay."

"Were you strip-searched?"

"Yes. Why?"

"Oh my God! You shouldn't have been! Do you know that it's illegal to strip-search a pretrial detainee?" She went on to tell me emphatically that she had always trained *everyone* under her that it was absolutely illegal to strip-search a pretrial detainee, and she wanted to know who the corrections officer was who did it. I told her it was Brandy, and she said again "Oh my God, she should have known better! All those girls know that they're not supposed to strip-search a pretrial detainee."

I figured it must be something important for her to get so excited about it, so I made a mental note to look it up later, and maybe ask Ron about it if he was in a decent mood.

Debbie then said *she* had something to tell *me*, but she was asking that I didn't repeat it to anyone else. I said, "Sure, no problem. What is it?

"I filed a lawsuit myself against Sheriff Brad Mason and the county." I started asking her questions, and I wasn't sure what she was talking about. She told me that she had alleged wrongful termination, that Brad Mason had been overheard saying that "no woman" would ever hold a position under him as deputy warden, and that he was determined to get rid of Debbie as soon as he took office at the beginning of the year. She said she was let go right after he was sworn in. She didn't seem to understand a lot of the details about her own suit but did tell me that it was a sex discrimination suit.

She asked me, "Do you think I'll win? Do you think I'll get anything?" She told me she had already paid thousands of dollars to a lawyer to file the suit, that she couldn't really afford it, and that she hoped it would eventually be worth it. She asked me, "What do you think my chances are?" I told her I wasn't all that familiar with discrimination cases, and what I had been studying and learning was all about Section 1983 civil rights cases, so I wasn't going to be very helpful in giving her my opinion or advice. I did tell her I was very glad that she had the courage to at least try to go after them, and told her how glad I was I had run into her, how good it was to see her.

When I went back to the office, I took the time to go on to the district court website to take a look at her case, but I couldn't find a thing with her name on it. I decided she must have filed it in another court or jurisdiction. I was sure it wasn't at the county level, because I knew they wouldn't deal with sex discrimination cases, and it had to be a federal suit.

I would later find out that she settled her lawsuit against the County for $30,000.

I would also later—much later, as in 2015—find out that former Sheriff Brad Mason was criminally charged for corrupting the morals of a seventeen-year-old girl who had been a tenant in one of his rental properties. Yes, Brad Mason is married and has a family.

~ ~ ~

I have attached a copy of the Pre-Trial Detainee Strip Search Form No. 1 (PD-1), which was given to me by Brandy Colley, the CO who booked me and strip-searched me. You will see that it clearly states that the CO has to "identify specific factors which establish reasonable suspicion that the Pretrial Detainee possesses a weapon, evidence of a crime, controlled substances or other contraband. Check all that apply."

Brandy Colley did *not* check any that applied, because there was none that applied.

And then she strip-searched me, humiliating me beyond description.

Date: 11/02/2007

Name of Pretrial Detainee

Brandy L. Coney

Name of Corrections Officer

Identify specific factors which establish reasonable suspicion
that the Pretrial Detainee possesses a weapon, evidence of a
crime, controlled substances, or other contraband. Check all that
apply:

_____ a. The appearance and demeanor of the detainee;

_____ b. The nature of the criminal charges pending against
the detainee;

_____ c. The detainee's prior arrest record (if known);

_____ d. Discoveries from prior arrests and/or prior search
of the detainee (if known);

_____ e. Detainee's conduct during the period of confinement;

_____ f. Detainee's known relationship with another inmate
and/or detainee;

_____ g. Detainee's known history of suicide attempts or
threats;

_____ h. Any other reasonable suspicion based upon specific
circumstances that leads the corrections officer to
suspect that the detainee is concealing weapons,
evidence of a specific crime, controlled substances
or other contraband.

Please describe: _____

_____

_____

Brandy L. Alley
CORRECTIONS OFFICER SIGNATURE

APPROVED BY:

_____   Date: _____
(DEPUTY) WARDEN   Time: _____

Depositions

Debbie Morlock sat across the conference table from me. I was there alone, after having spent weeks preparing my questions and doing more research, and she was seated next to the county's high-priced lawyer, Pat. Debbie repeatedly lied, under oath, and did it all with a smile. I could literally feel my head blow up like a balloon and was sure it was going to explode while I sat there. I was shaking, nauseated, and had such a pain in my head I could barely see.

Debbie told us all how I did "really well" while I was in jail, and she just never saw me sick, and never saw me despondent or hysterical, and that I seemed to her to be "happy" when she brought her little dog in for a visit one afternoon. What Debbie didn't say, or didn't care to see, was that when the other inmates were passing Debbie's little dog around, I had tears rolling down my face and I had to turn away. The pain I felt and the fear for my animals at home was unbearable. Debbie testified that she would often check on me to make sure I was doing okay and that she even checked to make sure I had money in my account, because she would have put some in herself if she knew I didn't have any. She said she did that regularly for other inmates!

I listened to Debbie put forth the most amazing self-aggrandizement I've ever heard in my entire life. I came to believe she is one of a handful of people that will tell you that they *once* thought they were wrong, but then found out they were mistaken. Just Perfection.

When I was in jail I had no money when I was sick, and at one point I was able to get a message to my friend (the one who never came to see me) that I needed some cash to buy soup from the commissary. Debbie stopped in at the cell block one afternoon to tell me that she had just seen my husband out in the lobby and that he had deposited $25 in my account so I could buy some things I needed for my "cold." When she referred to my husband, she said, "He makes me sick!"

But when it came time for her deposition, Debbie didn't remember anything. Like telling me how there had been an epidemic of MRSA or hepatitis in the jail, or that me being strip-searched was a violation of federal law, or that she had sued the county for wrongful termination, or anything. Debbie just couldn't remember *anything*.

Debbie and her husband had been clients of my husband's more than once, and we had briefly talked about how much we both loved real estate, and entertained the idea of having our own real estate agency someday with my husband as a broker. I guess it's a very good thing that we never followed through on that idea, because I don't sit well at my desk when I have a knife sticking out of my back, and I'm sure that's what I would have ended up with.

~ ~ ~

Tim Woodruff

Tim Woodruff was a different story. He knew nothing about my entire six-week incarceration period. He just knew *nothing*. And he was the warden!

Well, I take that back. When I asked Tim if he knew that it was illegal for me to be "punished" in his jail while I was still a pretrial detainee and had not been found guilty of anything, he very clearly stated that I had *never* been punished in "his" jail. He said I couldn't have been, because he never saw the purpose of his jail as one of punishment but, rather, as a place of "rehabilitation." So he said I *couldn't* have been punished. When I asked him what he thought being on lockdown for forty-eight hours in a five-by-eight-foot cell was defined as he responded that surely I understood that I was part of the population and had to be restricted like everyone else.

Yeah, that's it.

After a few hours of attempting to get some truth out of Debbie or Tim, I literally stumbled out of the courthouse, leaving the lawyer Pat Carey and his clients with big smiles on their faces. I went home and sobbed for hours, and my husband just told me I should have known better.

And I already knew better that my husband would never have sympathy or empathy for me then, because he never had.

~ ~ ~

The Judicial Conduct Board of Pennsylvania

In August of 2009 I filed three separate official complaints with the Judicial Conduct Board of the Commonwealth of Pennsylvania in Harrisburg against Judge John M. Cleland, district magistrate Dominic Cercone, and Judge Robert Saxton.

I was initially contacted by Frank Puskas of the Harrisburg office, and regularly corresponded with him at the onset of the "investigations" into my complaints. I sent him a copy of my twenty-one-page narrative outlining what had been done to me and my animals, and after he had read it, we had a long discussion about his thoughts and suggestions. He told me that my narrative "read like a Lifetime movie," and that he was so very sorry. He told me that he would do everything he could to keep on top of my case, and advised me to continue to send him any further information that would support my claims against the three judges.

I thought Mr. Puskas was a very nice man, and I thought he was genuinely concerned about me. I honestly thought Mr. Puskas was going to help me expose what had been done, and that he meant what he said. Mr. Puskas had told me that his mother-in-law also rescued animals, and that he really understood my anguish at what had happened to mine.

My case was eventually "transferred" to an investigator at the JCB, Douglas Miller, who worked out of the Pittsburgh office. I spoke several times with Mr. Miller, and he also reassured me that his office was going to aggressively pursue my allegations and complaints against the three judges.

Douglas Miller wanted to "interview" my husband in support of my complaints. My husband knew everything that had happened, and knew what my allegations were against the judges. He also knew that my allegations were all truthful, as he was present during the majority of their actions, or had firsthand knowledge otherwise. I was on the one hand hopeful that he would be truthful, and on the other hand, terrified that it would be a disaster, depending on his mood when he was interviewed.

Mr. Miller set up a time to talk with Ron at the office one afternoon, and I was in the adjacent room, listening to my husband's side of the conversation.

My heart again sank to the floor when I heard my husband say, "Yes, my wife has had mental health issues for years. Yes, my wife has been on medication for years."

I had been married to this man for twenty-two years at that time, and I knew that he had never, absolutely never, stood up for me or had my back, or attempted to defend or support me. Why I thought he would start then is something I can't answer, but I prayed that he would. He did not.

I tried to tell myself that I didn't need his help, and that somehow God was looking out for me, and that the truth would come out without him, and these men would be called to account for their actions against me. *Somehow.*

~ ~ ~

I began to be suspicious of how much investigating the JCB was actually doing, or going to do, when I was repeatedly told that any results of their investigation would be confidential, and that after personally interviewing the judges, no one was going to let me know what they had said, or what their positions were.

Over the course of more than a year, I wrote dozens of letters to the JCB, always furnishing them with copies of any and all supporting documentation. Sometimes many weeks or months would go by without a word from them. I finally got notice that my formal complaints were going to be heard by the Judicial Conduct Board in Harrisburg and that I would be notified of their findings after the hearing.

One afternoon, in mid-August of 2010, I looked in my mailbox and saw three letters on the ivory-colored stationery from the Pennsylvania Judicial Conduct Board. My heart pounded like it always did when I had news from a court. I could barely breathe, and I started shaking. *Please, God! Please let this be the news I've waited to hear!*

I opened the first envelope.

Dear Mrs. Langella:

The Judicial Conduct Board has completed its review of your complaint. The Board has asked me to advise you that it has dismissed the Complaint.

After conducting the necessary inquiry and upon careful consideration the Board has determined there was insufficient indication of judicial misconduct to justify further inquiry.

The Judicial Conduct Board's decision is final and there is no appellate process applicable to review the Board's disposition of a filed complaint.

The Judicial Conduct Board thanks you for taking the time to make your complaint known and appreciates your concerns for integrity and independence of the judiciary.

Very truly yours,
Joseph A. Massa, Jr., Esquire, Chief Counsel

~ ~ ~

Grief. Pain. Agony. Over a year of supplying them with supporting documentation of everything I had alleged. Cercone had falsified official court documents to keep me imprisoned, and they had copies. John Cleland knew about my husband's addictions, and knew that I was being kept in jail without due process or equal protection, and they had access to transcripts and court records. Saxton had belittled me in open court several times and had used fraudulent numbers provided by my husband to deny me any reasonable spousal support.

I just screamed and sobbed for hours until I had no energy and no more tears.

It had all been a sham, a hoax. The "Judicial Conduct Board" was never set up or intended to protect the public from corrupt judges. Its primary role and objective *was*, and *is*, to protect corrupt judges from the public. Period.

A New Suit

I had been struggling greatly to try to hang on with my federal suit against the county. The stress was so much worse than I ever expected, although I knew that trying to go it mostly alone was going to suck. I kept telling myself I could be strong enough to see them through until there was some resolution because I *had* to. I still had to find a way to be able to take care of my rescues and myself on my own, and there was no way to get free of my husband without money. Just no way. I literally prayed day and night that somehow God would move someone—some lawyer or judge or insurance company—to settle with me and pay me enough money to allow me to leave with my animals.

It just wasn't happening, and my husband's mental health issues were getting so much worse. I lived again with constant threats, four-letter words being spat at me, and fears of him figuring out some other way to get rid of all of us.

My husband still had many clients who were criminal defendants. He still knew his way around the court system very well, and when he applied himself, he could do a really good job. I would often make small talk with his clients when they came to the office to see him, and I started hearing a pattern from many that had recently been incarcerated in McKean County.

There appeared to be an epidemic of some kind of skin infection, and I say epidemic because everyone that I talked to either knew someone that had contracted it, or they had contracted it themselves. I decided to contact as many current inmates as I could by requesting weekly inmate population reports from the county, which I had to pay for. I wrote one form letter telling them that my husband and I were interested in helping them if they had run into any issues with serious health problems while they were incarcerated. I also addressed the issues of pretrial detainees being punished, and the fact that the law clearly stated that pretrial detainees had to be segregated from those who had been convicted of a crime.

I was really stunned by the number of letters I got back. All handwritten, and all sounding very sincere. Day after day I received new letters with the same theme. Most of the letter writers had contracted the same skin infection, and many had also developed other serious illnesses that weren't being treated.

One inmate literally had a mouth full of abscesses from bad teeth. When he was released a short time after writing to me, my husband and I met with him. He told us how he had to use a paper clip to pierce the swollen infections in his mouth to drain them because the jail couldn't—or wouldn't—get him to a dentist. He said they were only "allowed" to take a certain number of inmates for dental appointments every so often, like every couple of weeks, and they told him that there were no "emergency appointments." He described pain that I could only imagine.

Several other recent inmates came to our office and either took pictures themselves with my camera or let us take pictures. They had what looked like big boils or abscesses, some that were draining. On many different parts of their bodies, but most often on their torsos. Stomach, sides, under their arms. Really hideous-looking and sickening.

My husband advised every one of them to see a doctor immediately, and they all did.

What we discovered over several weeks, and after paying for and obtaining copies of their medical records, was more than sickening and disgusting. They had all contracted MRSA (methicillin-resistant Staphylococcus aureus), a bacterial infection that is extremely difficult to treat because, as its name suggests, it is very resistant to typical treatments.

Almost contemporaneously, the new sheriff/warden, Brad Mason, had been interviewed by the *Bradford Era* and had clearly stated that not only did they (the McKean County Jail) not presently have any issues with contagious diseases, but that there had not been any issues with contagious diseases in the recent past.

More importantly, we discovered that each and every one of them had been *lied* to, by both the "prison nurse" and the "prison doctor." They were told many different stories about what was wrong with them when they sought treatment while still incarcerated, but it was *never* that they had MRSA. They were often given antibiotics that were not appropriate for the treatment of MRSA, and they were always lied to.

From our interviews with the inmates, I remember vividly the story Debbie Morlock (the former deputy warden) had related to me in Walmart quite some time before. She had told me that an inmate had written to her and begged her to go to the men's cell block to see him. She said he was very sick, and when she pulled his hair back, she knew right away that he had MRSA. She said she threw a fit and "got him out of there" right away, sending him to the hospital. She told me "things like that happened all the time there" (at the McKean County Jail).

One of the most despicable aspects of what was going on with the MRSA outbreak and the lying by the jail employees was what they were *intentionally* doing by lying.

They were intentionally sending inmates home—to homes with small children and babies, to homes with senior citizens, to homes with pregnant women or diabetics, to homes with relatives or friends that were sick or frail or who had compromised immune systems, and intentionally risking infecting them as well through their deceit.

MRSA can be fatal. We learned of several people that had died in our area directly as a result of a MRSA infection as we investigated the inmates' claims.

My husband was convinced this was going to be the biggest case the county had ever had to defend, and I know he saw it as his personal vengeance. He was determined to file a class-action suit against the county, the medical staff, Sheriff/Warden Brad Mason, and the jail employees. He was convinced that he was going to expose more than just the MRSA epidemic and the lying. He was going to expose so much more that he knew about the McKean County Jail.

I wanted to believe he could do it. I knew he had the basis for a class-action suit. I knew he had victims that were willing to be lead plaintiffs. I knew we had all the medical records and the inmate records and all the proof we needed that they were being lied to on a regular basis. We had laid out a lot of money to put everything together and give them notice that the inmates were going to sue.

I wanted to believe he could do it, and I was terrified that he couldn't. I was the only one who knew how sick he was, and I was the only one who understood that he could barely function most of the time. I had to run the ball for so much of his work, and I was just about in pieces myself. I was still doing all the housework and taking care of our rescues, trying to work on my own lawsuits, do all of the office work, and now I was trying to advance these claims.

One evening my husband seemed to be in a reasonably stable state of mind and said he wanted to discuss the lawsuits with me. He told me that he was *convinced* that the suit on behalf of the inmates was going to settle for big money, and would then make him a lot of money. He told me he would gladly give it all to me. He told me he was "so worried" that I was so stressed and upset by my own cases, and he just "couldn't stand" to see me suffering over everything anymore, and he begged me to settle my case against the county for "anything you could get." He kept saying "You're focusing on the wrong case." He said I was exerting all my efforts in the wrong direction; that the case for the inmates was the "big money" and my own case would still take so long I'd never survive it. I told him how afraid I was that he would not be able to handle the work himself, and he kept telling me that he was *very* motivated because it was against the county and he knew they had done so many horrible things to so many people. Including him.

I took several days to think about it. My health was really going downhill. I was not sleeping much, I had serious stomach problems all the time, and my hair and eyelashes were falling out. I kept thinking how nice it would be to just let it go, but I so desperately wanted to stay with it until the end. I honestly believed it was my last chance to get out with my animals and save us all from more harm.

I decided to take a chance that maybe, just maybe, he was telling me the truth, and that he really could handle it, he really could advance the case and I would see enough money to be able to leave. He not only agreed that he would turn over to me any fee he might get from the case, but he also drew up an agreement that we signed and had notarized to that effect. So after more than a year of being mocked and laughed at and belittled by the county's high-priced lawyer, and after more than a year of watching the *Bradford Era* refuse to print anything when I would win and splash headlines when rulings went against me, I took next to nothing to settle the case. And I cried a lot.

Within a couple of months, my husband totally lost interest in pursuing the case, even though we'd spent money we couldn't afford to advance it, and he left all the clients with whom he'd signed fee agreements out to dry. He just walked away. Like always.

Yes, I should have known better, like always. And I just always wanted to believe things would change, things would get better. And they just didn't.

Langella v. Cercone

Judge Cohill had ruled in the federal suit that Cercone's actions in 2007 were subject to judicial immunity, and I could not proceed with my case against him in that regard. But he had also ruled that Cercone's actions in 2009— when he terrorized and threatened me once again—were *not* subject to immunity. Judicial immunity only attaches when a judge has jurisdiction over the "victim" by virtue of a pending court case before him or her. In 2007, the simple assault charge filed by my husband against me was overseen by Cercone, so immunity attached.

But in 2009, there was *no* case before Cercone that involved me. Therefore, the judge ruled, immunity did *not* attach. He could *not* threaten me or abuse me or terrorize me. At least not legally.

After weeks of more research, I filed a civil action in McKean County Court against Dom Cercone for intentional infliction of emotional distress. I was absolutely sure it was a winning case, and I knew I'd do everything I could to fight it until he was held accountable for what he had done to us. I also believed that, since I was filing the case against him as a private citizen and *not* in his capacity as a judge, he would have to hire his own lawyer and pay for his own legal costs.

Right?

Wrong!

Shortly after Cercone was served with the complaint, I received an entry of appearance filed by the same taxpayer-paid-for lawyer who had represented him in the federal suit. She was going to continue to be paid by the taxpayers for what he had done to me in 2009, and Cercone would again get all his representation for free. Oh, and she would continue to be a bitch. Again, she didn't respond to phone calls or letters from me. I'm sure she believed she didn't have to because no court was going to make her. After all, she worked for the courts.

The first order of business in *Langella v. Cercone* was getting someone in the McKean County judiciary to appoint a judge for the case. What I never expected was what happened next.

Judge Richard Saxton was appointed to hear *Langella v. Cercone!*

This was the same out-of-county judge who had overseen the divorce and support cases between my husband and me, and the same judge who had sentenced me on the assault case. The same judge who had screamed at me in open court and had "awarded" me $175 a week in spousal support—enough to take care of my rescues. The same judge who had told me at my sentencing on the assault case that he was going to "make an example" of my case, and told me how angry he was *at my husband* for "using" the judicial system for a domestic dispute, and handed me a big fine and court costs and told me if I dared step out of line within the remainder of the year of my probation, I would spend the rest of the entire year in jail.

I started crying and shaking when I saw the order appointing him. I immediately filed a motion to ask him to recuse himself, citing all of the above. I contacted the Administrative Office of Pennsylvania Courts (AOPC, where Mary Butler worked) and begged them to remove Saxton and appoint someone who could be impartial.

The AOPC told me they would not remove him, and Judge Saxton refused to recuse himself.

Screwed again. How much longer could this kind of crap keep happening?

~ ~ ~

I did all the research and jumped through all the hoops. My "ace in the hole" was the ruling from Judge Cohill in federal court that Cercone was not immune from prosecution with respect to his 2009 actions against me. Over and over again I attached a copy of his Opinion and Order reciting just that.

And after months of doing all the right things and following all the rules and knowing that I had a winning case against Cercone...

Judge Saxton dismissed my case again, citing judicial immunity!

I had spent money and time I could not afford to spend or waste, and had agonized over every aspect of the case, and it was all for absolutely nothing because Judge Richard Saxton was as corrupt and egomaniacal as the rest of them.

Of course, the *Bradford Era* ran a story about my case against Cercone being dismissed by Judge Saxton. Of course they did, because I was the loser in the story.

~ ~ ~

I was not ready to give up. Not yet! I still had a chance to spend more time and money that I could not afford and try to appeal Judge Saxton's ruling.

More incredible stress, more research, more jumping through hoops. I paid the appropriate fees and filed an appeal with the Superior Court of Pennsylvania in May of 2011, and I waited, for months.

The Opinion and Order came down from the Superior Court on September 2, 2011, and I received it one week later.

When I opened my mailbox again and saw the envelope from the Superior Court, my heart raced, and I nearly passed out. I was so terrified to open the envelope to find out that I had lost again. I sat down in my car and opened it, praying and telling myself that God would get me through this no matter what it said.

And then I cried. The Superior Court agreed with me, and had remanded my case against Cercone back to the county court.

~ ~ ~

I have attached a copy of the Superior Court's Opinion and Order.

J. S48016-11

2011 PA Super 196

CATHERINE F. LANGELLA,   IN THE SUPERIOR COURT OF
PENNSYLVANIA

     Appellant

v.

DOMINIC A. CERCONE, JR.,

     Appellee   No. 1720 WDA 2010

Appeal from the Order of October 15, 2010 in the
Court of Common Pleas of McKean County, Civil
Division, No. 797 C.D. 2010

BEFORE: ALLEN, LAZARUS, and OTT, JJ.

OPINION BY LAZARUS, J.:   FILED: SEPTEMBER 2, 2011

Catherine F. Langella appeals from the order of the Court of Common Pleas of McKean County, dated October 15, 2010, sustaining Dominic A. Cercone, Jr.'s preliminary objections and dismissing her complaint with prejudice. We affirm in part, reverse in part, and remand for reinstatement of Langella's complaint.

Dominic A. Cercone, Jr. (hereinafter "Judge Cercone") is the Magisterial District Judge for District Number 48-1-01, located in McKean County, Pennsylvania. On October 22, 2007, Catherine F. Langella (hereinafter "Langella") was charged with simple assault[1] and harassment[2] for striking her husband, then the McKean County Chief Public Defender. Langella was

---

[1] 18 Pa.C.S.A. § 2701.

[2] 18 Pa.C.S.A. § 2709.

arraigned before Judge Cercone, a colleague and friend of Langella's husband, who set Langella's bail at $5,000.00 unsecured. Langella posted bail the same day and was released.

On November 2, 2007, Langella's husband reported that Langella violated the conditions of her bail and Langella was arrested. That afternoon, Langella appeared for a hearing before Judge Cercone, who revoked her bail.

Langella alleges that during the November 2 hearing, she attempted to testify that she had not intentionally violated the terms of her bail, but Judge Cercone told her to "shut up." Appellant's Complaint, 6/15/2010, at ¶ 5. When Langella pleaded with Judge Cercone to allow her to go home to care for her more than forty rescue animals, Judge Cercone told her she had "more important things to worry about than her cats" and remanded her to jail. *Id.* at ¶¶ 6-7. Langella was then transported to the McKean County Prison where she served forty-two days.

During Langella's time in prison, Judge Cercone denied Langella's requests for a preliminary hearing and reinstatement of bail, and, according to Langella's complaint, falsified an official court document that kept her in prison without conviction or legal representation. Langella was finally granted a preliminary hearing on December 12, 2007. During the hearing, Judge Cercone threatened Langella with involuntary commitment to a psychiatric facility. Langella subsequently saw a psychiatrist who determined that no psychiatric commitment was necessary. Following the evaluation, Langella was allowed to return home, at which time she found her home destroyed and many of her rescue animals dead.

Two years later, on December 9, 2009, Langella contacted Judge Cercone's office to ask for an appointment with the judge. At 1:00 PM that afternoon, Langella met with Judge Cercone in his chambers in Bradford, Pennsylvania, and spoke with him with one of his secretaries present.

Langella began to speak with Judge Cercone about his actions toward her during the 2007 hearing, but Judge Cercone abruptly stood up and escorted Langella out of the office into the lobby. Langella avers that Judge Cercone then stated to his office staff, "I think [Langella] is having another episode. I think she needs to be committed. I think we should call Stoney (Greenman)."[3] *Id.* at ¶ 17.

Langella subsequently filed a Section 1983[4] suit in the United States District Court for the Western District of Pennsylvania naming Judge Cercone as a defendant. In evaluating Judge Cercone's motion to dismiss Langella's complaint, Senior District Court Judge Maurice B. Cohill, Jr. distinguished Judge Cercone's actions in the 2007 criminal proceeding from the 2009 meeting with Langella. *See Langella v. Cercone*, No. 09-cv-312E, 2010 WL 2402940, at *1 (E.D. Pa. June 10, 2010). Judge Cohill ruled that Judge Cercone's actions in 2007 were conducted within his judicial capacity and were, therefore, protected

---

[3] Stoney Greenman is a mental health professional.

[4] 42 U.S.C. § 1983.

by absolute judicial immunity. *See id.* at *8. As to Judge Cercone's actions toward Langelia in 2009, Judge Cohill found that the actions were not undertaken in a judicial capacity and were therefore not protected by judicial immunity. *Id.* Nevertheless, Judge Cohill dismissed Langelia's complaint, ruling that Langella's allegations of verbal abuse, threats and harassment, without any reinforcing act, were not actionable under Section 1983. *Id.*

On June 16, 2010, Langella filed a second complaint against Judge Cercone in the Court of Common Pleas of McKean County alleging a civil cause of action for intentional infliction of emotional distress based on his actions in 2007 and 2009. Judge Cercone filed preliminary objections in the nature of a demurrer. The Honorable Richard N. Saxton, S.J., sustained the demurrer, holding that Judge Cercone's actions in both 2007 and 2009 were within his judicial capacity, and thus protected by judicial immunity.

Langella filed a timely appeal on May 13, 2011. Langella raises the following issues for our review:

> 1. DID THE TRIAL COURT ERR IN SUSTAINING [JUDGE CERCONE'S] PRELIMINARY OBJECTIONS AND DISMISSING PLAINTIFF'S COMPLAINT?
>
> 2. WAS [JUDGE CERCONE] ENTITLED, AS A MATTER OF LAW, TO JUDICIAL IMMUNITY WITH RESPECT TO THE CLAIMS RAISED IN PLAINTIFF'S COMPLAINT?

> The relevant scope and standard of review in examining a challenge to an order sustaining preliminary objections in the nature of a *demurrer* are as follows:

> > Our review of a trial court's sustaining of preliminary objections in the nature of a *demurrer* is plenary. Such

- 4 -

> preliminary objections should be sustained only if,
> assuming the averments of the complaint to be true,
> the plaintiff has failed to assert a legally cognizable
> cause of action. We will reverse a trial court's decision
> to sustain preliminary objections only if the trial court
> has committed an error of law or an abuse of discretion.
>
> All material facts set forth in the complaint as well as all
> inferences reasonably [deducible] therefrom are
> admitted as true for [the purpose of this review]. The
> question presented by the *demurrer* is whether, on the
> facts averred, the law says with certainty that no
> recovery is possible. Where a doubt exists as to
> whether a *demurrer* should be sustained, this doubt
> should be resolved in favor of overruling it.

Lerner v. Lerner, 954 A.2d 1229, 1234 (Pa. Super. 2008) (internal citations omitted).

"[J]udges are absolutely immune from liability for damages when performing judicial acts, even if their actions are in error or performed with malice, provided there is not a clear absence of all jurisdiction over subject matter and person." *Feingold v. Hill*, 521 A.2d 33, 36 (Pa. Super. 1987) (citing *Stump v. Sparkman*, 435 U.S. 349, 356-57 (1978)). Thus, judicial immunity requires a two-part analysis: first, whether the judge has performed a judicial act; and second, whether the judge has some jurisdiction over the subject matter before him. "The rationale in support of such protection is that for magistrates to exercise their discretion freely and apply their understanding of the law to the facts before them, they must be granted such a measure of independence that they are not compelled to respond in damages for mistakes

- 5 -

J. S48016-11

honestly made provided they have not acted beyond the pale of their authority." **Beam v. Daihl**, 767 A.2d 585, 596 (Pa. Super. 2001).

In determining the limits of judicial immunity, courts have attempted to draw a line between "truly judicial acts, for which immunity is appropriate, and acts that simply happen to have been done by judges." **Forrester v. White**, 484 U.S. 219, 227 (1988). "[T]he factors determining whether an act by a judge is a 'judicial' one relate to the nature of the act itself, i.e., whether it is a function normally performed by a judge, and to the expectations of the parties, i.e., whether they dealt with the judge in his judicial capacity." **Petitioner of Dwyer**, 406 A.2d 1355, 1361 (Pa. 1979) (quoting **Stump, supra** at 362). Thus, administrative, legislative or executive functions of a judge, even if assigned to the judge by law, are not regarded as purely "judicial" acts, and are not entitled to judicial immunity. **See Forrester, supra** at 227. For actions taken by judges outside of the regular legal proceedings, the courts have looked to four factors that support a finding that a judicial act is involved:

> (1) The precise act complained of . . . is a normal judicial function; (2) the events involved occurred in the judge's chambers; (3) the controversy centered around a case then pending before the judge; and (4) the confrontation arose directly and immediately out of a visit to the judge in his official capacity.

Harper v. Merckle, 638 F.2d 848, 858 (5th Cir. 1981) (citation omitted).

Langella's claim of severe emotional distress arises from Judge Cercone's actions toward her in the 2007 criminal proceedings and the 2009 meeting, each of which requires a separate analysis of the issue of judicial immunity.

- 6 -

Judge Cercone's presiding over the 2007 criminal proceedings is a judicial function that falls squarely within the category of protected judicial acts. *See Forrester, supra* at 227 (judicial resolution of dispute between parties in court allows for uncontroversial application of judicial immunity). Further, all of Judge Cercone's statements during the proceeding, including his alleged falsification of a court document, were made within his jurisdiction to preside over criminal proceedings. *See* 42 Pa.C.S.A. § 1515 (statutory authority conferring jurisdiction to magisterial district judges in all criminal proceedings). That Judge Cercone allegedly acted with prejudice and malice in performing these judicial acts does not eliminate the protection of judicial immunity. *See Feingold, supra*. Accordingly, Langella's claim against Judge Cercone for his actions in 2007 are barred by judicial immunity.

Judge Cercone's 2009 meeting with Langella presents a more difficult question regarding the limits of judicial immunity. After careful review, we find that Judge Cercone lacked jurisdiction over the subject matter before him and that his actions were not judicial acts.

First, judicial immunity does not protect Judge Cercone because he lacked jurisdiction over the 2009 matter. Where there is a clear absence of jurisdiction over the subject matter and person, judicial immunity will not attach. *Feingold, supra* at 36. The facts here reveal a clear absence of jurisdiction. When Langella met with Judge Cercone in 2009, she was no longer a party to any action before the judge, and she did not go to discuss any legal matter before the court. Instead, she met with Judge Cercone to discuss a personal matter regarding a case decided two years earlier. A judge does not automatically obtain jurisdiction over a person merely because the person enters the judge's chambers to discuss matters ancillary to a prior decided case. Therefore, Judge Cercone lacked jurisdiction over Langella in the 2009 meeting.

Second, judicial immunity does not protect Judge Cercone because the 2009 meeting did not involve judicial acts. The trial court cites the Supreme Court's decision in *Mireles v. Waco*, 502 U.S. 9 (1991), to support its finding that Judge Cercone's acts were protected under judicial immunity; however, the facts of *Mireles* are distinguishable from the present case. In *Mireles*, the Supreme Court held that judicial immunity barred suit against a California Superior Court judge who ordered police officers to use excessive force to bring into his courtroom a lawyer who had failed to appear for a pending case. *Id.* at 10. The Court reasoned, "[a] judge's direction to court officers to bring a person who is in the courthouse before him is a function normally performed by a judge." *Id.* at 12. Further, "[the lawyer], who was called into the courtroom for purposes of a pending case, was dealing with [the judge] in the judge's judicial capacity." *Id.* Thus, *Mireles* recognized that a judge's actions, even if excessive, are protected by judicial immunity if they serve a judicial function. *See id.* at 13 ("[T]he relevant inquiry is the "nature" and "function" of the act, not the "act itself.").

- 8 -

Here, unlike *Mireles*, Judge Cercone was not engaged in a function generally performed by a judge when he met with Langella in 2009. Langella was not involved in any case pending before Judge Cercone when she went to meet him in his chambers, and Judge Cercone was not adjudicating any legal issue. Additionally, unlike *Mireles*, Judge Cercone was not acting in an official capacity because the meeting with Langella was personal. Thus, the issue here is not that Judge Cercone's actions exceeded the protection of judicial immunity, but that judicial immunity does not apply.

The factors adopted by the Fifth Circuit in *Harper*, *supra*, reinforce our analysis of *Mireles*. Although the second factor from *Harper*, that the events occurred in the judge's chambers, weighs in favor of judicial immunity, the first, third, and fourth factors all weigh strongly against it.

The first factor is not satisfied because the precise act complained of here, that Judge Cercone told Langella she needed psychiatric help in front of his office staff, did not arise out of a normal judicial function. Judge Cercone made these statements during a personal meeting, unrelated to any legal matter before the judge, and they did not further any function required by his role as a judge. *See Forrester*, *supra* at 227 (judges are not entitled to judicial immunity for acts that serve a non-judicial function, even if the act is a necessary part by the job).

The third factor is not established because the controversy did not center on any case pending before Judge Cercone. Langella's criminal case had concluded two years earlier and Langella was not involved in any other action before the court.

Finally, the fourth factor is not met because the confrontation did not arise out of a visit to the judge in his official capacity. Langella asserts in her complaint that Judge Cercone was a friend and colleague of her husband's for nearly twenty years, and that she went to visit Judge Cercone for personal reasons to determine whether he "expressed any regret, remorse or sorrow for his actions of 2007." Appellant's Complaint, ¶¶ 5, 14. Accepting the averments in the complaint as true, Langella did not intend to meet Judge Cercone in an official judicial capacity. *See Stump*, *supra* at 362 (expectations of parties is factor in determination of judicial act). Therefore, Judge Cercone's actions during the meeting were not protected judicial acts, and judicial immunity does not apply.

Accordingly, we affirm the order of the trial court as to Judge Cercone's actions in the 2007 criminal proceedings, and reverse and remand as to his actions in the 2009 meeting with Langella.[5]

Order affirmed in part and reversed in part. Case remanded for further proceedings consistent with this decision. Jurisdiction relinquished.

---

[5] Our holding is also consistent with the policy underlying the judicial immunity doctrine. "Immunity is . . . a solemn and sacred trust that should not be abused, and it is not to be regarded as a license for the judiciary to engage in improprieties." *Matter of XYP*, 567 A.2d 1036, 1039 (Pa. 1989). The purpose of judicial immunity is to encourage judges to freely exercise their discretion in applying the law without fear of personal civil action. *See Beam*, *supra* at 586. The 2009 meeting with Langella did not involve any activity by Judge Cercone that would justify special protection. Judge Cercone was not deciding any issues in a case currently before him, or considering the application of any law. Judge Cercone was merely meeting with Langella for what she believed was a personal matter, for which no immunity should attach.

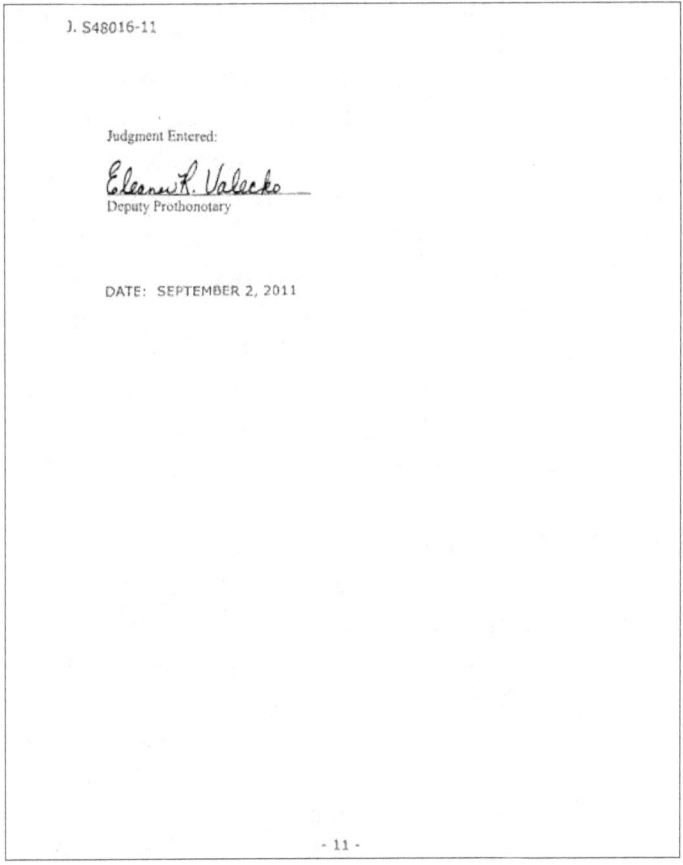

J. S48016-11

Judgment Entered:

Eleanor R. Valecko
Deputy Prothonotary

DATE: SEPTEMBER 2, 2011

- 11 -

I faxed the Opinion and Order to the *Bradford Era* that same day. The *Bradford Era* never ran any article or story about the reinstatement of my case. That's because I had won this time and their friend Dom Cercone had lost.

The *Legal Intelligencer*

Shortly after the decision came down from the Superior Court, I was contacted directly, and totally out of the blue, by a reporter at the *Legal Intelligencer*, a publication that apparently prides itself on being "the oldest law journal in the United States." He had seen the decision that had remanded my case against Cercone back to the county court and told me he was extremely interested in the details and background of the case. He wanted to publish an article in their next issue, and I was so excited and hopeful!

Over a period of weeks, I sent this reporter more than a hundred pages of supporting documentation. He continued to seem very interested, and kept encouraging me to give him more and more information, which I certainly did.

As I said, I was *so* excited and hopeful!

The *Intelligencer* did run a short, concise, and accurate article. When I would e-mail the reporter with updates on the progress of the case against Cercone, I wouldn't hear back from him most of the time. Eventually he told me that the paper was small and they had "very limited" resources, so he didn't know how much more time he could afford to give my story.

He apparently decided he couldn't give my story any more time at all, because he stopped responding to my e-mails, and I never heard from him again.

I should have known, but I was apparently still a genius.

~ ~ ~

Once I could breathe again, I realized that I had another nearly insurmountable hurdle to clear. My complaint against Cercone was going to again be overseen by Judge Saxton. How in the hell could I hope to get anywhere this time? I knew Judge Saxton would be enraged because the superior court had said, very clearly, that Judge Saxton was wrong. They backed up my position all along. I knew he would be thinking, *How could a man seated on the bench be proven wrong by a worthless female?* (like me). I knew what his opinion of me was. He had made it clear every time he had ridiculed me or shouted me down or sneered at me in open court.

But I jumped through more and more hoops and kept doing my best to advance my case. Cercone's lawyer filed a pleading that demanded I do something within a certain amount of time.

I asked my husband what the next step was going to be, and he told me that Judge Saxton would schedule a hearing on Cercone's pleading and would give me a time frame in which to respond.

I waited for a notice of hearing from Judge Saxton, and instead got a fist in the face for the zillionth time.

Judge Saxton ruled that I had not responded to Cercone's pleading within the amount of time Cercone's lawyer said I had to respond, *and Judge Saxton dismissed my case against Cercone.* Judge Saxton never scheduled a hearing on the pleading. He just figuratively raped me, again. I cried in anguish for hours. I had again spent so many months working so hard to fight for myself and my rescues, and it was again all in vain.

I could not do it any longer. From that day on, I had made up my mind that I would write a book, no matter how long it took, even if it killed me, and I would let everyone know just exactly what had happened.

There was no way for me to prevail in McKean County. No way in hell.

The Disciplinary Board of Pennsylvania

I have long understood that anyone who practices law, in any state, will invariably have complaints filed against them with the disciplinary board of their state. The DB is supposed to keep lawyers in check. Oversee them. Handle complaints against them and make sure they remedy the situation the best they can. Or punish the lawyers if they find that they've actually committed some wrong against a client.

Sounds good. If that was really what they do, then that sounds like a good thing. I can tell you, from years of personal experience, from years of reading every complaint that was filed against my husband, that the DB of Pennsylvania (and most likely all of the others) wants nothing more than to be able to dismiss as many complaints as they possibly can. Typically, the client is required to fill out a complaint form and file it with the board. The board then contacts the attorney with the narrative of the client's complaint and asks the attorney to provide the board with a complete explanation of what they feel happened. They usually take the attorney's explanation as gospel, and send a letter to the client telling them they really appreciate that they contacted the board, and that the board has determined that the attorney provided a reasonable explanation. The board will most often tell the client that the complaint against the attorney has been dismissed, and that all details of the complaint must be kept confidential.

In the early years of my husband's law practice, most of the complaints filed against him were honestly without merit. They would usually come from clients involved in divorce or disputed custody cases where the client vehemently disagreed with the outcome of the case. They felt that they got screwed. They then tried to say that their lawyer was the one that screwed them, and they wanted their money back. Very much like the criminal defendants you hear about who will say that they took a plea agreement that their lawyer *forced* them to take (doesn't happen), or that their lawyer didn't explain to them exactly what they were agreeing to (only happens when the person doesn't listen and isn't going to agree no matter what).

In the beginning, almost all of the complaints filed against him were like that, and almost all were dismissed out of hand. But as the years went by and my husband's physical and mental health continued to deteriorate, the complaints became more serious. He was becoming more and more detached and withdrawn, and more and more a captive of his addictions. He would often forget deadlines or ignore them. He would often become bored with the work he had been paid to do, and I would have to fight with him to get him to do it. This started long before our lives had descended into full-blown insanity. It started long before he had a heart attack in 2006.

I wrote directly to the Disciplinary Board's counsel, Sam Napoli, on numerous occasions. I told him that the complaints they were receiving were going to continue to get worse and more serious. I reminded him many times that I knew my husband far better than they ever could— far better than anyone.

I *begged* the Disciplinary Board to mandate that my husband get professional help for his addictions and for his mental health issues. I told them I wanted permission to speak at his next disciplinary hearing. The last year he practiced, he had to go to Pittsburgh more than once to answer to the most recent complaints. I told Mr. Napoli and the board, again and again, that the mistakes would increase and the complaints would continue as long as they refused to make him get help.

Sam Napoli and the board ignored me. *They* knew better. They never even suggested that he get any mental health treatment, let alone mandate it; and my guess is that they didn't because they were not going to admit that one of their own could possibly be mentally ill. He just had to be devious and dishonest and a typical lawyer.

And so the mistakes increased, and the complaints increased, and the board finally recommended that he be suspended from practice for one year. They made their recommendations to the Supreme Court, who in turn suspended him from practice for *five* years. My husband's career would be over, because he would turn sixty when the suspension went into effect.

He was now left with a debilitating mental illness, no job, no income and no prospects. If any of his enablers—from Dr. Bazzoui to Mike Olearchick to the Disciplinary Board—had ever really gotten "real" with him and stopped trying to be his friend, and had given him a "treatment or else" mandate, maybe he would gotten the help he needed years ago, and maybe he'd still be an attorney in good standing and a healthier, contributing member of society. But there was no way in hell he was going to listen to his wife when everyone else was giving him a pat on the back and feeling sorry for him.

~ ~ ~

Escape from McKean County

In October of 2011, my mother died in a hospice in Florida. She died believing that I was everything my husband had told her I was. Sick, pathetic, a gambling addict, and a thief. Worthless to anyone and a burden to my husband and family. She also died believing I was the reason she never had a day of happiness. In my heart, I have always known that is how she felt. My mother hadn't spoken to me since the week after I was released from jail in 2007, when she told me she felt sorry for my husband for having to live with me.

~ ~ ~

Toward the end of 2011, I was miraculously able to convince my husband that we—my rescues and I—needed to move out of the area. He was becoming more and more dangerous to me and to my animals, and I was also able to convince him that he would be happier if he had lots more "alone time" when he could eat what he wanted and watch the TV programs he wanted, and he wouldn't have to listen to me. He could stay in the little makeshift apartment I'd set up in the back of the office, complete with a mini kitchen, a futon, and a shower. I told him I would still do all of his work using GoToMyPC on our computers and he could come "home" on weekends.

I had to believe that moving to an area far removed from McKean County would be so much safer for me because he would have no ties to any corruption somewhere else. I was sure he couldn't convince other judges or law enforcement to go along with him wanting to harm me.

And so I found a wonderful lease-to-own house, most assuredly through divine intervention, and spent several weeks driving my rescues to our new home, a few at a time. I took responsibility for the entire move and making improvements to accommodate our animals. I just had to believe that I was being given a chance to get away from the evil that is so prevalent in what seemed to be godforsaken McKean County.

I was able to live in peace like I'd never known, and thanked God every single day for one more day of safety. One more day without screaming and threats and four-letter words in my home. I would wait on him hand and foot when he was home on the weekends and make sure he was occupied and as happy as was possible for him. I did whatever I could to make sure my animals and I were safe. Well, almost anything. I was no longer a prostitute wife.

~ ~ ~

By the end of 2013, he felt his life was in ruins, and he said he had nothing left to be thankful for. He told me he often felt he was dying. He was now spending more than twelve hours a day in front of the computer with the office doors often locked, blinds drawn, phone going unanswered, mail piling up on the desk unopened. He would visit me on weekends and became more and more nervous about making the trip because he was becoming more and more afraid to drive. He had multiple accidents with the car and would often not tell me.

I ultimately found out that he hadn't been paying the rent on the office for nearly a year, and he was being evicted from the place that I'd spent many weeks and a lot of money renovating and redecorating when we first rented it. It was in the best location and was the most perfect office we'd ever had. It wasn't because he didn't have the money to pay the rent. He always had enough money to pay the rent, but didn't tell me he was "forgetting" to pay it. I had been driving to the office once every two or three weeks to check on things, and every time I was there I would find more than thirty unlistened-to messages on the always-full answering machine. The mail would be stacked up on one of the desks, mostly unopened.

I tried to encourage him that Christmas was coming and we could just spend a few days having some peace and quiet, and he could be away from everything. Maybe get some rest. On Christmas Eve, about lunchtime, he called me, sounding more than despondent.

He said, "I have something to tell you. Something really bad happened."

I could not even imagine what else "bad" could have happened.

He told me he was on his way out the door to get some breakfast and was confronted by two sheriff's deputies. They told him a bench warrant had been issued for his arrest, and that they had orders from Chris Hauser to pick him up and transport him to the courthouse.

It was Christmas Eve. He was handcuffed and put in the back of the sheriff's car and was driven to the courthouse. He was escorted into the courtroom to face his longtime "friend" and former Dickinson School of Law classmate Chris Hauser, who was sitting on the bench.

He was told that he had missed a hearing on a divorce case the day before and that he was being held in contempt of court. My husband said he didn't know there was a hearing scheduled for December 23, the day before. Of course he didn't know. All of his mail was unopened on the desk. The notice had been sent, and he had never seen it. Instead, he was at the hospital undergoing a stress test with his cardiologist while the hearing was held. He failed the stress test and was told that he needed to undergo another cardiac catheterization as soon as possible.

His "friend" Chris, the criminal judge, ridiculed him in open court, and then made reference to his pending license suspension. Chris told him that he must have been able to convince the Supreme Court that there was mitigation to get them to change their minds, because he couldn't understand why he wasn't yet suspended. He told my husband that he had been "watching" the Supreme Court activity for his suspension order and had not yet seen it.

He received the notice of his suspension within the week, just after Christmas.

It was probably the best thing that ever happened to him in his entire life, bar nothing.

My husband could not go lower than he was, and it was absolutely what he needed. No more enabling, no more coddling, no more excuses.

Shortly after he lost it all, he agreed to get help. Because I had relocated to a big city, we had access to the most amazing medical care. Because we were nearly penniless, he had access to Medicaid, which paid for all of that amazing medical care. When he first started getting help, he was diagnosed as barely functional, at 35% to 50%, with bipolar depression and a host of other mental health problems. He not only got wonderful care, but now he had access to medical professionals who would take the time to work with him to trial-and-error him on the right medications, and not just hand him a bag of pills and slap him on the back.

Although he applied for Social Security Disability, he was initially turned down, and an appeal took nine months before he prevailed. We nearly lost our home several times because we couldn't pay anything on the lease and were only able to survive by borrowing from a few amazing, caring, and compassionate friends and selling nearly every single thing we owned that was worth anything. When we saw we were running out of food for our animals we took our flat screen TVs off the walls and sold them on craigslist—for a low-enough price that I knew they would sell the same day. I sold everything from my kitchen that wasn't a necessity, and he sold his sports collectibles. He spent weekend after weekend standing in our driveway throughout the spring and summer selling whatever we could, no matter how small. We dug through junk drawers and boxes in the garage to find things we might get a dollar for.

One of the hardest things for him to do was to e-mail his former law school classmates and literally beg them for help. He had not come to terms with his illness being in any way comparable to having cancer or some other serious health problem. He felt a lot of embarrassment and humiliation. He struggled mightily with feeling like a failure while hearing about how his old friends were doing well in their careers. It was very hard, but also very good in many ways.

I'd like to be able to say that the people who could most afford to help him *did*, but they did not. Chris Hauser was now making more than $160,000 a year as a judge, devoid of character and morals and ethics as he is, and never offered him a dollar. Not as a loan, not as a gift. Not anything.

On the contrary, when Chris Hauser heard about my husband's suspension, he immediately went to the law school e-mail string and posted a pathetic, almost-cheering note about how this was a "sad and tragic day for Ron, and I am sure he would appreciate receiving some words of encouragement from all of you." He never gave him any "words of encouragement" himself. He also went on to tell my husband's friends that my husband hadn't paid his rent on the office and that he suspected he wasn't taking his medications. How he could have known that is a real mystery!

What a great man that Chris Hauser *still* is!

Getting Personal

In McKean County, Pennsylvania, there is an obvious, almost incestuous and corrupt relationship between just about everyone in a position of power or authority. There are no "islands"; there is almost no one with a mind of their own. That is the biggest reason no one spoke up when I was imprisoned illegally, or when my animals were being abused and neglected. They all had to protect each other.

John Cleland could have stopped what was happening to me and my rescues, very early on in our torment. To the best of my knowledge, he never asked a question about why the chief public defender's wife was imprisoned for weeks without hearing or bail. He knew my husband was an addict, and Judge Cleland knew that he had to protect the county from liability issues and potential lawsuits.

John Satterwhite could have stopped what was happening to me and my rescues, also very early on. He had more information than just about anyone else, and it would have only taken him publishing a story or printing pictures of the devastation in my home, and I would have seen dozens, maybe hundreds, of local animal lovers come to our aid.

Greg Henry and Chris Hauser could have easily refused to help my husband with his request to do what they could to keep me imprisoned.

And of course, *Dom Cercone could have said "No!" to Chris Hauser or my husband or anyone else and sent me home with a warning.* Dom Cercone knew I was not a flight risk. I wasn't going anywhere with dozens of rescue animals to care for. I hadn't taken a real vacation in fifteen years, and I never let my animals go without care.

On the following pages, I will give you a few more details about those people who harmed my rescues and me. You should readily see the links between all of them.

Greg Henry

Greg Henry was a classmate of my husband's and of Chris Hauser's at the Dickinson School of Law in Carlisle,

Pennsylvania, graduating in 1979. Over the course of more than twenty-five years, I heard dozens of stories about Greg from my husband and many of their classmates. Greg was well known for excessive drinking, excessive womanizing, and various forms of mistreatment of many young women.

Greg always seemed to have a Svengali-like control over many females, and it was always lost on me that although most women knew of his history of mistreatment and abuse, they still seemed to be enthralled by him. For years he dated a female bar owner that would eventually ask him to help her sue a state trooper, and it was public knowledge that he was involved in multiple physical altercations with her. He was never charged with abuse or simple assault or harassment or *anything*, to the best of my knowledge. The only time I was aware that he was charged criminally was when he bit another man in the stomach at a local bar while he was mayor of the City of Bradford. And women were still captivated by him after that!

Chris Hauser's secretary was one (married) woman that was obviously completely taken by Greg. They would have lunch together nearly every day when he was in town, and she would defend both Greg and Chris to the ends of the earth. Everyone in the local legal community knew that Cindy was always right behind Greg, dreamy-eyed, and that she even did extra work for him as often as she could.

A young (married) female attorney who often discussed cases with my husband was also smitten with Greg, and seemed totally mesmerized by him. It was again common knowledge that she saw Greg as one of the most intelligent men she'd ever known. She is now the presumed district-attorney-elect in McKean County, and I absolutely expect that she will name Greg Henry—the alcoholic, womanizing, lying, abusing con man that he is—to the position of assistant district attorney when she takes over the office.

When I was desperately trying to literally "fight City Hall" over caring for feline rescues in our neighborhood, Greg was the city's attorney, and was responsible for all of the pleadings and paperwork to attempt to prosecute me. I had invited Greg to come to my house so he could see our rescues and how well they were being cared for, and so he could see for himself where I was caring for the outside homeless animals, in an outbuilding that I had heated and where they were protected from the harsh winters. After seeing, with his own eyes, that the representations of our neighbors were untrue, and that we had spent a lot of time and money trying to do everything "right," he went back to the city and proceeded to pound me even harder in court.

Actually, Greg had given suggestions to the city for punishment for me if I continued to care for the homeless animals outside on our property. I would face a $200-a-day fine, and if I continued to defy their order that I completely stop feeding or caring for the homeless animals, they said they had the right to come onto my property and tear down my outbuildings! My garage and a heated workshop!

When a rescue group from Pittsburgh read about my battles with the city over the homeless cats, they contacted me and told me they wanted to help. They explained to me that they had been working with the city of Pittsburgh and had been very successful at doing TNR (trap/neuter/return) and lots of other methods of maintaining feral cat colonies. One of their members was a senior professor from Duquesne University. They wanted to testify at the hearing before the mayor, the City Council, and the city's attorney, Greg Henry.

These wonderful people spent their own time and money and drove from Pittsburgh to Bradford, bringing more than a dozen bags of cat food with them that had been donated, and went to City Hall with me. On the advice of their counsel, Greg Henry, the City of Bradford refused to even let them testify. Even better, our former mayor, Michele Corignani, stated, "If you people came here to tell us how to care for feral cats, I can tell you right now I'm *not* interested in anything you have to say!" (Can you guess that Michele and Greg were good friends? Yes, they were.)

~ ~ ~

The worst story I've ever heard about Greg Henry—far worse, in my opinion, than when he assaulted girlfriends—is that he had actually lit a cat on fire when he was a teenager and had laughed about it. I heard that story from a woman who went to school with Greg and knew him growing up.

No wonder he had no sympathy for the homeless and abandoned animals I had been caring for! He only saw them as combustible entertainment—*not* innocent, living creatures!

When my husband's health had seriously declined and everything in our lives had been seriously unraveling, Greg took disgusting advantage of my husband's state of mind by using him to bail him out of dozens of work projects that he had ignored. Greg knew that we were in dire need of additional income because my husband had mistreated and neglected so many of his own clients that he was getting less and less new work. We were really hurting, and Greg really needed help. He would routinely call my husband, at the very last minute, and tell him that he was up against the wall, that he was sorely behind and going to be in serious trouble, and could he help him, like *now*? Like *today*? My husband would come back to our office with piles of files, saying we had "emergencies" that had to be worked on *immediately* for Greg. Often we would have to work evenings to try to catch things up for him. Greg always promised him payment of fees he was either holding or that he would be getting imminently.

I was constantly arguing with my husband that I knew Greg often lied to him, and would promise him over and over that he would give him a nice fee for the extra work but would often stiff him, sometimes for weeks at a time. In the end, I couldn't argue that we really needed the money, and so it was worth the risk that we would do the work and hope against hope that we would get paid.

For most of 2013, Greg mentally and emotionally abused my husband to the point where he would just come back to the office and withdraw for days. If he was especially irate, he would just take it out on me, along with everything else, and would never say much to his "best friend." He was afraid to stand up to Greg because he was afraid he would stop giving him work, and he just couldn't handle Greg lying to him. He had always known that Greg often lied to his own clients, but he could not understand how Greg could call him a friend and mistreat him so badly.

When my husband and I decided to "reconcile," a mutual friend of ours told us both that Greg had been drinking heavily at a local restaurant ("heavily," even for Greg) and that he told our friend that he had just lost his best friend because his "best friend" had just gone back to his wife.

How sad and pathetic.

One of the most abusive relationships Greg has ever had was—and most likely still is—with a male friend of mine that I've known since grade school. Somehow Greg induced him to become somewhat of a "manservant" to him, although

I believe a much more appropriate word would be *man-slave*. I know that my friend often needed money and Greg went so much beyond taking advantage of him it would make any normal person sick. He regularly used him as a lackey—a servant, a flunky. He would send him off on the most menial of tasks and would invariably scream at him when he didn't perform to Greg's standards. Keep in mind that this man is my age, not a young boy. We're talking in his fifties and sixties when he was taking this crap. And most likely still is. My heart really broke for him so many times, but Attorney Svengali somehow had control over this meek and goodhearted man and abused the hell out of him. Most likely still is.

When my husband would say "I don't understand what's wrong with him," I would always, *always* respond, "Greg is an alcoholic. Period. You shouldn't need any other explanation."

My husband and Greg's relationship devolved into an abuser/enabler situation. We would do work for Greg, and my husband would hand-deliver it to him, sometimes on the same day. Greg would then tell him what day, and what time *specifically* to stop in at his office and he would pay him. He would go to Greg's office after hours or on a Saturday or Sunday, exactly when Greg told him to come, and nine times out of ten, the doors would be locked, and he would refuse to answer the phone, even though his car would be parked out in front of his office building. When my husband would eventually talk with him on the phone or see him on some later date, he would always have some extremely pathetic, lame excuse, so much more juvenile and asinine and unbelievable than any ten-year-old kid's excuses.

"I'm sorry, I guess I wasn't paying attention."

"Sorry, I guess I didn't hear the phone."

"Sorry, I guess I must have been engrossed in something."

"Sorry, I guess I forgot."

And then he would tell him he had another project for him so he could make some extra money.

~ ~ ~

When Greg learned that my husband was going to be suspended, he kept telling him that he didn't want him to leave town. He kept promising him he was going to get him a job doing collections for the city (Greg was still city attorney) and that he would also help him find some office space, maybe in his own building. Greg made those promises to him for months, and for some sick reason, my husband still wanted to believe that he was telling the truth. He kept telling him he was getting things "lined up," and my husband kept hoping. I knew that little of what Greg had ever promised him ever panned out, and that he just loved being not only the center of attention, but also loved my husband seeing him as some kind of "source" for just about everything he needed. He loved it when someone *begged* him for something. He loved feeling like he was in control of someone else's life, and I'm sure it's mostly because he never felt in control of his own.

I know this may be hard for many people to believe, but Gregory Henry is probably one of the most insecure and incapable people I've ever met. Incapable of having an honest relationship, incapable of putting another human being ahead of himself, incapable of telling the truth. A real pathological liar. A devious man who didn't blink an eye when my husband asked for his help in "punishing" me and my innocent, helpless animals.

My husband never could have tortured or harmed me and my animals without the one-on-one, hands-on assistance of Greg Henry.

And Chris Hauser.

Chris Hauser

As I have said previously, my husband went to the Dickinson School of Law in Carlisle, Pennsylvania, with Chris Hauser and Greg Henry. When my husband and I reconciled, he told me, very specifically, that Chris Hauser had called Dom Cercone himself to ask Dom to "do what he could" to keep me in jail as long as possible. *Collusion. Illegal. Evil.* My husband also told me that he had a conversation with Greg Henry about the request to keep me imprisoned, and that Greg assured him that "Chris has taken care of it."

Just imagine what *else* "Chris has taken care of" since he became a judge!

Chris Hauser was *not* a stellar student, and was also *not* a stellar lawyer. He had a very mediocre, very limited practice with a firm that represented mostly wealthy clients. Chris never did much get-your-hands-dirty legal work, like family law or criminal law or anything that would have been beneath him. He married late in life, fulfilling the prophecy that he'd never marry unless he found someone with money, which he did.

Interestingly, a quote from a *Bradford Era* article in 2009 in which Chris announced his intention to run for the second judgeship in the county read as follows:

> A common pleas court judge has a responsibility to protect the rights of all citizens. He must apply the law wisely and with complete impartiality.

I guess that only applied to whomever he *chose* to treat with impartiality, not really *all* citizens. Oh yeah, and he wasn't technically a judge yet, so what he did to me didn't actually count anyways. My husband's colleagues and friends all knew that the law wasn't going to be applied to me in any impartial or constitutional way. I was going to be stripped of all of that silly impartiality and constitutionality.

Yeah, that's it.

~ ~ ~

When I was sent to jail I was in the middle of working on a second house flip I had undertaken for some investors. I had been very successful on the first flip I did for them, and they got a check for over $22,000 after all of our expenses were paid. I was excited beyond description when I finally believed that I had found something I was good at that was totally separate and apart from my husband, and was so sure that it was going to provide me a way out.

After catching up with piles of past-due bills and giving substantial money to my daughter, the only things I bought for myself out of my proceeds were some really nice new power tools—a sliding compound miter saw and stand I'd been drooling over for a couple years, a table saw, and a few other tools. When I was arrested and put in jail, all my tools were at the jobsite, at the second house I was flipping for my investors.

When I got home from jail, one of the first things I thought of trying to sell was my miter saw and stand. I had paid almost $700 for them, and since they were nearly new, I figured I could get enough that would really help me for a while. I made some phone calls to some contractors and posted some messages on the local Internet provider's ad space. When a guy called me and said he was interested in buying them, I asked him to give me a ride to the jobsite where the tools were located.

He did, and when I went to the front door of the house and put my key in the lock, it wouldn't open. The locks had been changed, and *all* my tools were inside!

I was frantically making phone calls, trying to find out what had happened. The guy who gave me a ride and was interested in buying my tools dropped me off at home and told me to forget about it.

I contacted the township police that had jurisdiction over the jobsite, and would soon find out what had happened. My investors' lawyer was Chris Hauser! He had told them to change the locks on the property, and he also told them not to let me have my own tools!

Shortly thereafter, I received a letter from Chris Hauser himself, telling me that he believed I had purchased my new tools with "gambling winnings," and that he felt my husband had an interest in them, so he wasn't going to advise anyone to let me have them.

To make a very long story short, I did not get my tools back for more than six months, and "visited" the township police department more than a dozen times, always leaving in tears. Every single time, the township police would tell me that Chris Hauser advised them not to let me have my own property.

This is the man about whom I desperately tried to warn everyone in McKean County! *This* is the man who was still elected second judge in McKean County because low-information voters had no idea who he really was!

When Chris announced that he was going to be seeking the second judgeship in our county, I did everything I could possibly think of to try to get people to know just exactly who he was. I tried to follow any speeches or appearances he planned to make. When I would ask the organizers to let me speak at any of those events, I was always turned away. I knew better than to try to barge in somewhere because it would be another one-way ticket for me back to jail, I was sure. I wrote letters to the McKean County Republican Committee sending them copies of documentation I had about everything that had happened to me, and repeatedly told them that Chris Hauser had asked Dom Cercone, on my husband's behalf, to keep me locked up without a hearing. I told them that Chris had advised his clients, my investors, to keep my own tools from me. I told them that Chris Hauser had set my husband up in an apartment while our rescue animals were suffering and dying in our home. I *begged* them to stop him from running. I told them that I knew he was dangerous and could harm many others if he was given that much power and authority.

~ ~ ~

Super Bowl Sunday 2008
(Part 2)

On Super Bowl Sunday in 2008, when I had gone to the alleyway to try to retrieve my own car from where my husband had left it, there was no "incident," until Barb (Greg's secretary and Chris' former lover) called my husband and he showed up, telling me I was going back to jail for violating my bail conditions. I had removed the air filter from my own car and had otherwise done nothing to anyone. Nothing at all.

I received the following letter from Chris Hauser a few days later, threatening me with arrest.

CHRISTOPHER G. HAUSER
Attorney-at-Law
78 Main Street, 4th Floor
Bradford, PA 16701
Phone: 814 362-5519
Fax: 814 362-8113
Email: chauser@atlanticbb.net
Also a member of the New York Bar

February 4, 2008

Mrs. Catherine F. Langella
236 East Main Street
Bradford, PA 16701

Dear Cathy:

I own the properties situate at 104 and 110 Congress Street, Bradford, PA.

I have been notified by several of my tenants of an incident that occurred on Sunday evening, February 3, 2008 at 110 Congress Street involving you, Ron and the police. This incident alarmed my tenants and placed them in fear for their safety. It has also raised a concern with them regarding potential damage to their personal property.

It is my responsibility as a landlord to ensure the safety of my tenants and their peaceful enjoyment of their rented apartments. Accordingly, you are hereby notified that YOU ARE NOT TO COME UPON THE PROPERTIES SITUATE AT 104 AND 110 CONGRESS STREET AND/OR ATTEMPT TO ENTER EITHER OF THE RESIDENCES LOCATED ON THESE PROPERTIES. I have advised my tenants to call the police and to have you arrested for criminal trespass if you violate this direction.

Very truly yours,

Christopher G. Hauser

CGH:clm
cc: Harold B. Fink, Esquire
      Bradford City Police Department
      District Judge Dominic A. Cercone
      Tenants
c:\cindy\ltr\langella-langella

As you can see from the letter, Chris refers to two different addresses in his letter. Although he did technically own them, I knew from conversations he'd had with my husband that he had overextended himself and his mortgage lender had been threatening foreclosure for quite some time. He had purchased and mortgaged two huge apartment buildings, fancying himself a real estate magnate, but not making ends meet. Chris had sought advice about the possibility of filing for bankruptcy.

When Chris set my husband up in his former apartment (by now Chris had moved in with his wife-to-be) my husband told me that it was full of very expensive things that he was sure Chris couldn't afford.

Of course, now Chris can afford anything. He was able to keep everything he had done to me from the voters until he was elected our second county court judge.

I have attached a copy of the letter I wrote to Chris the day after he was elected.

Catherine F. Langella
539 Bolivar Drive
Bradford, Pennsylvania 16701
(814) 366-7006 FAX (814) 362-6776

May 18, 2011

Christopher G. Hauser
78 Main Street
Bradford, PA 16701

Re: Primaries

Dear Chris:

I read with great interest your comments in today's paper. You "didn't think it would end like this", or something.

I have waited to see the outcome of the elections, praying that anyone but you would win, and I could not have to subject myself to more anguish and more stress in following through with exposing you.

In 2007, long before you were a judge-elect, you assisted your former law school classmate in keeping me in a jail cell, covered with bruises inflicted by my husband, for six excruciating and tortuous weeks, while my rescue animals were dying in my home. You gave my multiple-addicted husband an apartment where he set himself up with a new computer, downloaded more hard-core porn, joined online dating sites and pursued a female bartender for sex, all while he was legally married to me. You picked up the phone, calling Dominic Cercone, who had remanded me to that jail, and asked him to see what he could do to deny me bail or keep me in that cell as long as possible.

I know you did these things because my husband told me you did. I know you did these things because Mike Ward told me.

After I was released from that Hell, you instructed your clients, the Gardners, to keep my property from me, thousands of dollars' worth, knowing I had no legal representation, knowing what my husband was doing. It was not returned to me for more than six months. You implied that I had purchased my contractor's tools with gambling winnings. You were wrong, but it was nonetheless none of your business how I purchased them.

I know you did those things because the Township Police and the Gardners' attorney and my husband told me you did them.

You had no legal right to do all of the things you did to me and my innocent rescue animals. What you did to me was nothing less than criminal. Both you and Dom Cercone committed criminal acts and absolutely denied me my rights to due process and equal protection under the law. But you did them anyways. And now you believe that you will be given a position of such extreme responsibility and gravity and POWER and the community is to believe that you will not abuse such power. This argument is a no-brainer and a non-starter. I know well about the Doctrine of Judicial Immunity, and you could do to anyone else what Dom Cercone did to me, and much worse, and suffer no consequences.

I saw your cute little "infomercial" where you talked about the Constitution. Come on, Chris, what country's constitution were you referring to? North Korea's?

My life was ravaged and raped at the hands of my husband, you and your colleagues. If this community wants to install you in such a position of power and authority, it will have to be with the full knowledge of not only what you have done, but what you are capable of doing.

To a man, everyone that victimized ME has acted as if they were a victim. You included. Not one "man" has come to me with an apology, or any regret, remorse or contrition. I am forced to live with a man that is diagnosed with bi-polar mental illness and regularly threatens and abuses me and my animals. I live with daily flashbacks and nightmares and you believe you have walked away unscathed.

No, Chris, you still have to be held accountable. You are about to see yourself as a co-star in my online videos, and much, much more, and you can talk all day about what a criminal I am because I misappropriated funds years ago. There was no Constitutional law that said you, or my husband, or Dom Cercone, or Greg Henry, or anyone, could be my judge, jury and executioner. You all sentenced me and my rescue animals to horrific suffering, and even death, and you will not walk away without answering.

And beyond this life, you will absolutely not walk away without answering.

Isaiah 54:17. No weapon formed against me shall prosper.

Very sincerely,

Cathy Langella

/cfl
Cc: The Bradford Era
        McKean County Commissioners

Dominic Cercone

The voters of McKean County elected this "man" district judge.

I met Dom Cercone when I was married to my second husband. They worked construction together. I remember very well stopping at the house Dom shared with his first wife and their three sons. I remember that Dom had a big mouth and was a bully. I also remember being told that Dom and his wife were well known for having knock-down, drag-out fights. I don't recall Dom ever getting arrested or going to jail for hitting his wife, but I was told he hit her many times.

Dom Cercone went on to become a Bradford City police officer. Not too many qualifications required for that position, but I think being a bully and passing a test must have been two of them.

Dom Cercone later married a young woman who worked at – wait for it! – *The Bradford Era!* Pat Frantz Cercone worked at the newspaper for many years before leaving to take a job at the local university.

After I had filed my lawsuits against the county and Cercone, among others, I ran into a friend who told me that she was aware that Dom's wife, Pat, was deathly afraid of him. He was a bully, and he didn't want her out of his sight. This person told me that Pat's friends were very worried about her because Dom had taken complete control of her life and she was afraid to stand up to him.

So Dom Cercone was not only responsible for denying me due process and equal protection, but he also bullied and abused his own wife.

Why am I not surprised?

~ ~ ~

One of my favorite places to go to eat in the summertime in our area was the Tastee Freeze. My husband and I had gone there every summer for more than twenty years. But after I had been out of jail for some time and we would again go to the Tastee Freeze, I would often pull into a parking space there, and who would be standing at the window to order but Dom and his wife! I would just be overcome with terror in a split second. I could see myself in that cell and my home destroyed and my animals dying or dead. I could see Dom laughing at me when I told him that Jody would die without her fluids.

My first thought was always how much I wished I could step on the gas and ram him into the front of the building, and then my second thought was always *My animals need me*, and I would just have to sit there and endure the mental and emotional trauma while he laughed and joked with his wife or a friend.

Dom Cercone is a pathological liar, an abuser, a bully, and a criminal. And if the voters of McKean County continue to elect him, they will absolutely deserve what they get.

Martin Causer

Duly elected to the Pennsylvania House of Representatives and "serving" for more than ten years now, Martin Causer has an office in the same building that was once occupied by Chris Hauser, and is still occupied by Greg Henry. They were, and are, all friends. Causer was also friends with Cercone and the city police department.

In 2009, when I was desperately trying to contact our state and federal representatives and senators I stopped in to Causer's office several times, hoping to be able to speak to him in person. I had already sent him a copy of my twenty-one-page narrative and had followed up with several phone calls to his Bradford office.

As you will see by the attached letter from Causer, he pretends to think that I was asking him for help with a "legal matter."

That is a lie.

I repeatedly told him, in writing and in person, that many attorneys and judges were involved in harming me and my rescue animals, and I was begging that an investigation of our county be undertaken by Pennsylvania's House and/or Senate.

Causer goes on to say that he is "prohibited from becoming involved in the legal affairs of my constituents." I never asked him to become involved in any legal affairs. On the contrary, I was sticking under his nose proof that his "friends" had deprived me of all of my constitutional rights, and was asking that he either refer the matter to the Congress or to law enforcement.

Martin Causer was a self-serving liar whose only interests were (1) protecting his own job and taxpayer-paid-for benefits, and (2) covering the asses of his friends that had done very, very bad things.

I pray that people get involved in putting up an honorable, moral, and ethical candidate to run against him next time and send him home to Turtlepoint.

MARTIN T. CAUSER, MEMBER
HOUSE OF REPRESENTATIVES

PO BOX 202067
HARRISBURG, PA 17120-2067
PHONE: (717) 787-5075
FAX: (717) 705-7021

78 MAIN STREET, 1ST FLOOR
BRADFORD, PA 16701
PHONE: (814) 362-4400
FAX: (814) 362-4405

107 SOUTH MAIN STREET
ROOM 1
COUDERSPORT, PA 16915
PHONE: (814) 274-9769
FAX: (814) 274-9159

HOUSE OF REPRESENTATIVES
COMMONWEALTH OF PENNSYLVANIA
HARRISBURG

COMMITTEES

COMMERCE
FINANCIAL SERVICES & BANKING
  SUBCOMMITTEE CHAIRMAN
ENVIRONMENTAL RESOURCES & ENERGY
PARKS AND FORESTS
  SUBCOMMITTEE CHAIRMAN
POLICY
VETERANS AFFAIRS & EMERGENCY
  PREPAREDNESS

CAUCUSES

TIMBER CAUCUS, CO-CHAIRMAN
FIREFIGHTERS & EMERGENCY SERVICES
  CAUCUS, VICE-CHAIRMAN
SPORTSMEN'S CAUCUS
RURAL HEALTH CAUCUS
ALTERNATIVE ENERGY CAUCUS
OIL AND GAS CAUCUS

September 29, 2009

Mrs. Catherine Langella
232 Bolivar Drive
Bradford, PA 16701

Dear Mrs. Langella:

I am writing in response to your recent visit to my office on Monday, September 28th.

As I explained to you, I am unable to provide you with assistance regarding your legal matter. As a state representative, I am prohibited from becoming involved in the personal legal affairs of my constituents. Such involvement would be improper and would constitute an abuse of my office. Our Constitution clearly defines the powers and duties of the executive, legislative and judicial branches of government.

I realize this information is not what you sought in contacting me; however, it is important for you to understand that I simply cannot offer any assistance with this matter. You may be best served by seeking the advice and assistance of competent legal counsel.

Sincerely,

Martin T. Causer
State Representative
67th Legislative District

MTC

John Satterwhite, the *Bradford Era*, and Another Best Friend

I have already explained that John Satterwhite is the owner and publisher of the only local newspaper, and he absolutely refused to run any stories in his paper that would in any way incriminate the county or his friends and colleagues. He had absolutely no problem running front-page stories about me when I was on the losing end of a court battle, and even published details that my husband and I had gone through bankruptcy and were trying to save our home from tax sale. The same reporter who refused to help me when she knew I was being abused and deprived of my rights—Marcie Schellhammer—had also filed for bankruptcy protection with her husband around the same time. When I asked John Satterwhite if he wanted the details of Marcie's bankruptcy filing (information available to the public) so he could print it after he'd printed mine, he refused to answer me.

Marcie and her husband had every right to file for bankruptcy protection, as anyone does who has tens of thousands of dollars of credit card debt that they can't afford to pay back. And the *Era* had every right not to make it part of a story about me. Of course, they would always pick and choose what they deemed to be "newsworthy."

~ ~ ~

My other closest friend and I had been friends since grade school. When she was going through her own grief and heartache several years before, her husband, who was an alcoholic and was also a porn addict, had left her for a very young woman. I had tried to be there for her every minute I possibly could. I would change plans and drop everything so I could spend time with her when she was hysterical and falling apart. I loved her and was so worried about her, and I was deathly afraid she would hurt herself.

My friend had worked for John Satterwhite at the *Bradford Era* for several years, during times of many crises in her life. She would often tell me that John was "so good" to her because he was very worried about her too, and he would invite her out on his boat to get her away from things and give her a distraction. She obviously thought the world of him.

My best friend never visited me once in jail, refused my calls after I got home, and never spoke to me again. I had called her when I had finally been able to get an appointment at the welfare office to reapply for food stamps, and I left several messages begging her to give me a ride to my appointment, but she never returned my calls.

I can honestly say I never did a thing to hurt her, and always considered her one of the closest friends I'd ever had. It was devastating to me to learn that when "friends" tell you they love you and then they find out you're "damaged goods," they don't even know who you are.

I didn't understand it then, but I can only assume that it had something to do with John Satterwhite, her former boss and friend.

~ ~ ~

Long after I'd been out of jail and was spending every spare minute trying to find someone to represent me, trying to find someone to give me some publicity, I was eventually able to talk with John Satterwhite on the phone. I caught up with him in his office at the *Era*. I had already written to him several times, begging him to cover the story of my husband's abuse of my rescues, begging him to cover the illegalities perpetrated by Dom Cercone and Chris Hauser and the rest.

John Satterwhite told me, in no uncertain terms, that his newspaper would not print anything that had happened to me. He would not print anything about what had happened to my animals. John Satterwhite owned both the local newspaper and the *Olean Times-Herald*, to the best of my knowledge, and that was the only other newspaper of wide circulation in our area.

I had reminded John Satterwhite that he had been given a huge public trust, and that it was his sacred obligation to print the truth. His readers had a right to know what was really going on in their community.

After begging him one last time and praying there would be some sense of obligation and decency to print the real news, he refused again, and offered this piece of advice:

"Cathy, there are many *other* ways for you to get your story out. Why don't you try radio?"

I said, "Mr. Satterwhite, don't you own the radio station?" And he said, "Well, yes."

I said something like, "You've got to be kidding." And he said the only other thing he could suggest was the Internet. And then he hung up.

What Took Me So Long

I AM SURE that many people would ask me why I waited so long to write this book. Most of the harm that was done to me and my animals was in 2007 and 2008, although the threats continued until very recently.

I have several reasons. From the day I was jailed in November of 2007, I was acutely aware that my life was in danger. By the time I was released six weeks later, it was clear to me that I could have died in the McKean County Jail, and no one would have ever questioned why, or how, or anything. My husband would have had all of my rescues destroyed, he would have continued with his progressive addictions and would probably also be dead by now. No one would have ever been questioned, or asked to explain, or held to account for the terror and the torture that was inflicted on me and my innocent animals.

I knew I could not do this until I felt I was in a "safer" place. Out of the jurisdiction of the City of Bradford, the

County of McKean, Dominic Cercone, and the judiciary of the county. Out of the jurisdiction of the city police department, who would have continued to do my husband's bidding if he had asked them.

Although I have now been out of McKean County for more than three years, I am still dealing with the post-traumatic stress I have suffered since I was released from jail in December of 2007. All of a sudden, you're just *there*. You're where you never, ever want to be again. And it's really hard to get out of "there." You literally just want to run away from yourself. Run away from your own thoughts and the rushes of terror that overtake you. You can feel your blood pressure rise, face flush, heart race, you sweat, you shake, you get dizzy, you are afraid. And maybe you're just in your own home, surrounded by your own things, and you're just "there." Just like the trauma of rape never goes away, the trauma inflicted upon me by the "legal criminals" in McKean County has not gone away either.

~ ~ ~

More than three years ago, I determined that I had to do this, more than anything, for my innocent and helpless animals that lost their lives at the hands of "respectable" men who cared nothing for my suffering, or for the suffering of those innocent little creatures who had never hurt anyone. All they ever wanted was to be loved and cared for, as we all do. It was what I tried to do for them every single day of their lives until the day I was forced to abandon them at the directive of the lawyers and judges who became self-appointed juries and executioners—Dominic Cercone, Chris Hauser, Greg Henry, John Cleland, Debbie Babcox, John Satterwhite, and my own husband.

With the exception of my husband, not one ever asked me for forgiveness. Not one has ever admitted to doing anything wrong, of making a mistake, of looking the other way when they knew they should not have. The issue is not so much forgiving them for what they did to *me*. I cannot forgive them for what they did to the innocent animals that deserved *nothing* that was done to them. As far as I am concerned, they are no better than child abusers. Every single one of them knew, beyond a shadow of a doubt, that I had many rescue animals that I had been caring for, for many years. They have absolutely no content of character or ethics or moral authority that would qualify any one of them to be a judge or lawyer or police officer or anyone in any position of authority.

Something that has never been lost on me is how my husband was able to achieve what he did—keep me in a cell without hearings or bail, deny me spousal support, take my car and home from me, sell my personal property out from under me without my knowledge, file a petition to have my bail revoked, threaten me with involuntary commitment to a psychiatric facility, and on and on.

My husband *never* could have accomplished even *one* of those things without John Cleland and Dom Cercone and Greg Henry and Chris Hauser and John Egbert and John Satterwhite and Debbie Babcox and the Bradford City Police and the McKean County court system all working together to "help" him.

Honestly, they didn't want to "help" my husband. On the contrary, they couldn't have cared less than they did about him. What they cared about was the liability issue(s) to the county, and protecting each other. They had all been given proof, multiple times, that my husband was very sick, and that he was a pornography *addict*, not someone who just looked at other women as a diversion. They knew that he had been looking at teen porn, a felony in Pennsylvania. They knew he could have been dangerous to children or teenagers he represented in his capacity as an attorney for Children and Youth Services, or representing parents.

When I was in jail, he was called in for a meeting with the then-head of personnel for the County, Michele Alfieri. My husband would later tell me that she told him they needed "proof" that he "wasn't a danger to children." They put him on administrative leave for four weeks, he saw a "therapist," and that "therapist" determined that he "wasn't a danger to children." He was then allowed to return to all his regular duties for the county.

Wow! At that time I had lived with him for twenty-one years and the "therapist" knew him better than I did!

I guess that, even though I knew he had raging addictions, that "therapist" must have been able to "cure" him!

I don't believe for one minute that I was the only victim of these corrupt, power-hungry lawyers and judges. If they did these things to me—and everything that was done to me and my rescues is documented and can be verified—they would do it again and again and again. They probably already have. But maybe now they will be watched a bit more closely.

Or maybe they won't.

Where We Are Now

As I AM going forward with the publishing of this book, I am faced with many more challenges and struggles. We lost the rent-to-own house I loved because we weren't able to obtain mortgage financing after my husband's disability determation, and our landlords wanted the house sold to other buyers.

My husband's suspension from the practice of law was one of the best things that could have ever happened to him, but regularly living below the poverty line is not only very hard, but can be very uncomfortable. Knowing there won't be any big fees anymore isn't good news, but if he *hadn't* been able to get away from the corruption and get appropriate medical and psychiatric care, I am convinced that he would be dead. And I don't even want to think what *else* might have happened to my furkids and me.

Most importantly, I have learned that there was never one person I could completely trust. Not one. Not ever.

That has been heartbreaking for me. I have been told "I love you" by men that abused me, by men that left me, by men that didn't know what it meant. I have been told "I love you" by my relatives and my own daughters, and I now know that someone telling you "I love you" does not necessarily guarantee that the sentiment will last, or endure the tests of time. When someone tells you "I love you" they most often mean that they do *at that time*. That does not ever guarantee that they will love you tomorrow, or next week, or next year, and certainly does not guarantee a lifetime. Most people do not understand what it means to love unconditionally, and are not capable of it.

I didn't write this book to evangelize, but I absolutely learned that there was only One that would unconditionally love me *no matter what*. He would never condemn me or abuse me or abandon me, and unfortunately, for most of my life, I didn't think that was enough. I thought I had to be defined by a man that would tell me I was worthy of being loved, *or not worthy* of being loved, or honored or respected or treasured. The Rapist taught me, when I was 9 years old, that I was not worthy of being loved, and that I was nothing more than a means to an end.

I now reject that. I now know that I am loved unconditionally, and honored and respected and treasured. Not by a man, but by the One that created me, and created me for a purpose. For *that* I am so grateful!

~ ~ ~

Speak Up!

I KNOW THERE are countless people who have had some kind of personal experience with the McKean County Jail, the city of Bradford, McKean County law enforcement and the McKean County Judiciary (judges and lawyers).

I know that many people have been mistreated by the *Bradford Era*, and there are most likely many stories most of us haven't read or heard about because John Satterwhite and his staff refused to print them.

I know there are countless people that have had some kind of personal experience with the mental health system in McKean County, which includes the Guidance Center, Dr. Bazzoui, psychologists, therapists, counselors, and other psychiatrists. Dr. Bazzoui did and said some very inappropriate things to me over the course of many years, especially during the years he was divorced, and I know for a fact that there are many women in McKean County that had the same bad experiences with him. I know because

I've talked to some personally, and they all related stories so similar to mine that they just could not have been made up.

I also know there are countless people who have been victimized and harmed by one or more of these people. No one was ever going to listen to you, so you didn't bother trying to lodge a complaint or file a lawsuit. No one was ever going to "believe you over them," to paraphrase one of my husband's favorite threats. Most likely, no one was ever going to take you seriously, or even give a damn.

But now you are going to be listened to. Together we can make sure people hear us and listen to us, not just in McKean County, but across this country. The corruption and abuse of power that exists in northwestern Pennsylvania exists all over. We just don't hear about other places like they don't hear about us.

I have set up a Facebook page, "Judicial Terrorism," where I am inviting you, and strongly encouraging you, to post whatever you like. Let everyone know what happened to you personally. In the jail, in the court system, with your own lawyer, with your own mental health professional, with "the system," with the newspaper. Because of the wide-reaching miracle of the Internet, we can make sure we're not ignored any longer. Maybe we can even make a difference, and try to make sure these things don't happen to others after us.

Please let me hear from you. Let everyone hear from you.

We need to be constantly reminded that these people that have been entrusted with so much power and control are absolutely *no* better than anyone else, and never will be. But if they aren't stopped, the abuse and harm will continue, or get even worse.

My Furkids

For those of you that are animal lovers, on the following pages I have tried to give you an idea of just who my rescues are, and who they have been. And it is also so important that you know how much they meant to me. How much they mean to me today.

I have cared for more than two hundred rescues over more than fifteen years, and the majority of them are gone. Although I have held dozens of them while they took their last breaths, while they passed from this godforsaken place to someplace much, much better, I have not had the luxury of being able to grieve for many of them in years.

When I lose one of my little angels I tuck them away deep in my heart, and tell myself that, when this is all over, I will take the time to grieve. If I had allowed myself grief and mourning for them in the past eight or nine years, I would not have survived everything I've had to go through and do. I look into the eyes of the innocent animals that are still with me, and I know can't cheat them out of the best I can give them now, because I know that they too will soon be gone. It's always too soon.

Porky

Porky was one of a litter of feral kittens I'd raised since he was tiny. He was the sweetest little gray tiger boy, and he took to me from the time he was very young. He always seemed to be as healthy as the other cats and kittens, and I never worried about Porky.

For a very long time, I've believed that God sent me the rescues I took in because they gave me so much comfort and so much joy regardless of what kind of pain I was in otherwise. Regardless of what I was facing or dreading. Porky was like a little guardian angel to me. When I would be curled up on the couch sobbing and in pain, Porky was the first one that would jump up beside me and put his head on my shoulder. He always wanted to sleep up against my side and would just purr and snuggle, and the pain would be a bit more manageable. He always knew when I was really hurting. If he heard me crying he would come running and jump up beside me. Porky heard me crying a lot his whole life.

When Porky was about four years old, he got sick. Not a little bit at a time, but he got really sick all at once. Nothing was right with him. Within a day or two, he literally couldn't move. His whole body seemed to be paralyzed. He couldn't lift a paw or lift his head, but he was fully alert and aware and awake. I was terrified and so scared. I had taken care of so many animals for many years and had learned to do a lot of things myself to care for them. But I'd never seen paralysis, and I knew that what Porky had was going to cost a fortune to diagnose, let alone treat. We had many experiences with vets who insisted on lots of blood tests before they'd try any treatments, and we just couldn't afford it. I had so many other animals to care for, and if I spent a fortune on one of them for vet bills, I'd never have enough money to feed and care for the others.

And so I did what I usually did. I tried everything I could think of to help him, and promised him I'd never give up until he was better. I knew there was a really good chance he would die, but I wasn't going to say it.

And of course, I prayed a lot. Over the years, I saw many miracles in my furkids' lives when I prayed for them, so it was always a great idea and never a waste of time, no matter what happened. I knew, without question, that God had created them; and I knew, without question, that he was capable of healing them.

I had learned that one of the best go-to foods for sick cats is baby food. Meat baby foods. Chicken, ham, turkey. So I stocked up on glass jars of baby food, and three times a day, I propped Porky up on the couch, on his puppy pads, and fed him warmed-up chicken baby food. He would look at me as though he knew exactly what was going on, and he would enthusiastically swallow his baby food. I bought unflavored Pedialyte and would syringe it into his mouth with a dropper in between bites of baby food. I would have to hold his head up with one hand and feed him with the other. I would give him a couple blobs of NutriCal under his palate and wash his face with baby wipes when he was done eating. He had a great appetite, and I knew that as long as he was eating and drinking, we had a chance.

I eventually learned to use the smallest disposable baby diapers I could find and tape them around his little butt with a hole cut out for his tail. I would turn him many times a day because I was afraid he would get some kind of bed sores, or whatever an animal would get from lying in the same position too long. It was really humorous sometimes, but also heartbreaking. I had always seen my Porky running and jumping and playing around the house, and now he could only eat and drink and sleep. And purr, of course.

Porky and I spent great quality time together for four weeks doing all these things. He was surviving, and he seemed quite content, so I just kept taking care of him the best I could.

One day I came home from work and peered into Porky's room to check on him. Porky wasn't on his couch. He was lying on the floor on his side, about ten feet from his regular sleeping spot. He had dragged himself there somehow, but I have no idea exactly how.

And so I cried for Porky, and I was so happy! I put him back on his couch and fed him his baby food and Pedialyte and changed his little diaper and kept doing it for more than another week, and Porky kept dragging himself around until one day he didn't have to drag himself anymore. He was walking, and then he was running, and he told me he didn't want to wear any more damned diapers, so he decided to get better.

It was one of the most amazing things that ever happened in my life. A true miracle.

Two years later, Porky got really sick again, and I tried to do all of the same things for him. I had started writing this book, and I'd found it to be so hard, and so distressing, and I was praying and asking God to please not take Porky because I just couldn't handle it right now. But this time, Porky stopped swallowing his Pedialyte, or anything else, and Porky died on his favorite chair while I snuggled him.

And so, like so many others, Porky is now an angel; and I am sure he is at the Rainbow Bridge, running and playing and celebrating that he doesn't have to wear those damned diapers and waiting for his Mama to come and snuggle with him again.

Scooterpants

I adopted Scooterpants from the local SPCA when he was about six weeks old. He was pure white, long-haired, and very, very sick. The assistant manager of the shelter had asked me to please take him home with me. She told me he had nearly died twice, and that she had taken him home with her to try to treat him away from the sickness that was always so prevalent in the shelter. I already had eight rescues at home, and Scooterpants became number 9.

I didn't name Scooterpants until after I knew he was going to survive. He had to have special formula and NutriCal and eye drops and lots of attention. When he started getting better, he was a little spitfire, and because he was always running at top speed through our house, I realized he was "scooting" everywhere. Scooterpants.

Scooterpants was one of the most loving furboys you could imagine, and he had six toes on each "mitt." One of his favorite things to do was to stand on the kitchen table and put his mitts on your shoulders, getting his back scratched and head-butting you furiously, purring even more furiously.

Early last year, just after my husband had been determined to be disabled, during another time when we were struggling so badly just to survive, Scooterpants fell from a third-floor railing onto the landing on the second floor. When I first found him, I thought he was just lying on the floor at the bottom of the stairs, but when I called him to come to me, he didn't move.

Scooterpants had fallen too far and had damaged something in his back or spine. He was totally paralyzed, with the exception of being able to move his head. I was devastated, and I knew there was not going to be any good outcome for him. He was thirteen years old, and there wasn't anything we could even consider doing because we couldn't afford it. My husband was nearly crippled from his mental health issues, and I was already carrying all the work around the house and with the animals.

I fed Scooterpants jars of baby food, day and night, and he got Pedialyte and NutriCal, and he wore little diapers, like his "brother" Porky had years before. But unlike Porky, he didn't keep getting a little bit better; he just kept getting a little bit worse. I had to turn him many times a day, and although he was very alert and aware of what was going on, it was beyond heartbreaking to see him motionless. I could also see real frustration in his eyes. He had always loved to play and run and put his paws on my shoulders, and now he couldn't.

Scooterpants died three weeks after he fell.

Baby Weezie

One winter night in 2006, in the midst of the insanity in my house, I heard a knock at the front door. It was a real blizzard outside, and I couldn't imagine who would even be out in that weather, let alone stopping for a visit. I opened the front door and saw a man standing there I didn't recognize. I turned the porch light on and could see that he was holding something in his arms, but I wasn't sure what it was.

He told me he needed my help. I asked him what he needed, and he lifted his jacket and showed me a cat. A frozen cat. He said he had found it across the street at the convenience store—in a snowbank. It was barely breathing, but he said he knew it was still alive.

"Please help me. I know what you do. I've heard about how much you've done to help animals. Please do something to help me." I never asked him who he was or how he heard about me or my rescues. I just asked him to hand me the cat.

As soon as I looked at it, I was sure there was nothing I could do. It was not only covered in snow, but it had little icicles frozen to its eyes and around its mouth. He just looked at me again and said, "Please try!" And I said I would and shut the door. I never saw him or heard from him again.

I ran and got towels and wrapped up the cat. It was uncovered long enough for me to recognize it as one of the feral cats I'd fed and tried to care for outside. I knew it was a "she" because it was mostly white, but with calico spots. I had seen her trying to get up against the house to protect herself from the wind and cold, but I could never get near her. Like most of the ferals I'd ever cared for, she was never going to let a human being get close to her. They were all so deathly afraid of people.

Now she had no choice. She had no ability to run or do anything. She felt like a block of ice. I wrapped her in towels and called our vet's emergency service. He called me back within a few minutes, and I told him what I'd been asked to do. He told me there probably wasn't much I could do, but I could at least try to warm her up. He told me what to do to try to thaw her out without subjecting her to too much heat or hot water. I spent most of that night trying warm her up, wiping ice from her eyes and nose, and syringing water into her mouth.

And of course, I prayed. I knew it never hurt; and often, very often, it helped. I had known for years that God had given me whatever "it" was inside that made me look at animals and see their fear or sadness or loneliness. And for many years, I would often say that I wished he'd never given me the love or compassion for animals because it has caused me more pain and anguish in my life than just about anything else.

She was still alive in the morning, and that was a miracle in itself. One thing I noticed about her right away was that her eyes were wide open, and they just wouldn't close. Even when she seemed to be asleep as she warmed up, her eyes stayed wide open.

I gave her whatever I thought she could handle. Some water, some NutriCal, lots of warmth. She survived, sort of. I named her Baby Weezie.

Baby Weezie learned to love getting petted, and most of all, she learned to love breakfast and suppertime. She would sleep on the back of the couch—with her eyes wide open—on a baby blanket. As soon as she heard me start opening cans for meals, she would literally plunge off the back of the couch to the floor and out to the kitchen. She had learned not to be shy about getting her "fair share" of meals and would jump into the plate full of food and stand in it while she ate. When she was done, she would use her litter box and go back to her couch. She would purr when she was held or petted, and she was a happy little girl.

I also knew that Baby Weezie had brain damage from her near-death freezing. I was sure that was why her eyes never closed. And she lived a very limited little existence, never wanting to play or explore. She was just content to eat and sleep and be loved.

One morning, I came downstairs to fix breakfast and saw that Baby Weezie was having convulsions on her couch. I knew what was happening, and it just crushed me. I picked her up and wrapped her in a clean baby blanket and held her. I rocked her on the couch in my arms for what seemed like hours, and Baby Weezie died in my arms. Like I'd done dozens of times before, I sobbed and rocked her and whispered, "I'm *so* sorry! I'm *so* sorry!" My heart always broke into pieces when I would think of how little they wanted out of life and how much they loved when they found someone to care for them. There were just so many that were so cheated out of what they deserved.

Shortly after Baby Weezie died, I wrote a two-page story about her little life—she survived and was with me for about four wonderful months—and sent it to the *Bradford Era* and begged them to run her story on the editorial page. I knew that the Letters to the Editor column allowed only so many words, but I also knew that they regularly ran guest editorials where they made exceptions for length when they thought it was something timely or topical. I tried to explain, again, how much pain and suffering there was with so many homeless and abandoned animals in our community, and I said that I was sure I could reach more people who might not understand just how bad it could be. Maybe I could even get some people to help me.

John Satterwhite and the *Bradford Era* refused. And no one else ever heard about Baby Weezie—until now.

McKean County has more than its fair share of losers, rich, poor and in-between. So many people that are so self-absorbed they see helpless animals as nothing more than an inconvenience. Or fiery entertainment. Like Greg Henry.

~ ~ ~

You can see many photos of my wonderful furkids on my Facebook page. Each and every one was a tremendous blessing to me, and I would encourage anyone even considering it to *please* save a life and rescue a homeless animal! They will love you unconditionally and forever, and you will be more blessed than you can imagine!

—Cathy Langella